«... these forty years the Lord thy God hath been with thee; thou hast lacked nothing.»

Deuteronomy 2:7

«... Go home to thy friends, and tell them how great things the Lord hath done for thee...»

St. Mark 5:19

THESE FORTY YEARS

© 1981 por el autor, Robert Munn.

ISBN 84 - 7228 - 599 - 5
Depósito Legal: B. 16.577 - 81

Impreso en los Talleres Gráficos de la M.C.E.
Horeb, A.C. n.º 265. Galvani, 113. TERRASSA

Printed in Spain

Robert Munn

THESE FORTY YEARS

A testimony of God's faithfulness during forty years of active missionary service

Author: Trophies of Grace

CONTENS

PREFACE

On a number of occasions during our furloughs from the various mission fields where we have labored, when we have spoken in churches, conferences and camp meetings, many of our friends have come and said to us, «Why don't you share some of these experiences in a book so that others who may never hear you speak can at least read it and be challenged and blessed by it?»

As the years have passed and it seemed like we were fast approaching what might be the end of our active missionary service, we have felt led to do just that. So after a good deal of prayer and asking for God's help, we have endeavoured to share some of the great things the Lord has done for us whereof we are glad.

Our sincere prayer and the sole purpose of recording These Forty Years is that God and God alone will be glorified, because we know that we are only what we are because of His marvellous grace. Praise God!

7

One of our greatest joys that we have not mentioned in this record of God's faithfullness to us is that He likewise called our son, Jim, and his sweet wife, Lydia, to join the hundreds of other M.Ks. who have answered God's call and are seeking to fulfill the Great Commission and win for the Lamb the reward of His sufferings. To this great company of M.Ks. scattered through the mission fields of the world is this book affectionately dedicated.

D and D Missionary Homes
4020 58 Avenue, N.
St. Petersburg, Florida

CHAPTER 1

How It All Began

Is it possible to be called to missionary service before one knows the Lord as his personal Savior? The prophet Jeremiah and the apostle Paul would both answer in the affirmative. Jeremiah testified, «Then the word of the Lord came unto me saying, Before I formed thee in the belly I knew thee; and before thou camest forth out of the womb I sanctified thee, and ordained thee a prophet unto the nations.» (Jeremiah 1:4, 5)

The apostle Paul states in Galatians 1:15, 16, «But when it pleased God, who separated me from my mother's womb, and called me by his grace, to reveal his son in me, that I might preach him among the heathen; immediately I conferred not with flesh and blood.»

Both, undoubtedly, had a personal encounter with God. Paul's experience of conversion is clearly recorded in the Acts of the Apostles, chapter nine.

I remember coming home for a holiday in my second year of Bible College and finding a little missionary book in the attic. It was entitled, *Livingstone, the Pathfinder* by Basil Matthews. Casually opening it, I was amused to read under my name, written in childish handwriting, «Some day I shall follow in the footsteps of David Livingstone.»

I remembered having received this little biography for good attendance at Sunday School, and reading it several times as a boy. But I don't remember writing what I did on the flyleaf. I must have been about eight years old when I expressed my determination to follow in the footsteps of the great missionary pioneer!

Like Jeremiah and Paul, I also had a personal encounter with Jesus Christ. It may not have been as dramatic as Paul's experience on the Damascus road, but it was nevertheless as real.

In November 1931, Jock Troupe, a well-known Scotch evangelist, came to Belfast to conduct a three-week evangelistic campaign in Crosscollyer Street Evangelical Presbyterian Church. Our family always attended church services twice on Sundays and Sunday School in the afternoon. The same was true for every evangelistic meeting held in our district. We had no choice; Mother would take no excuse for not attending.

When the campaign began, my younger brother Fred and I were told, «You are going to the mission tonight to hear Jock Troupe.» On the way to the church, which was different from the one we always attended, we planned to do what we usually did in our own church on Sunday evenings—get a back seat, as far from the preacher as possible—and amuse ourselves, playing X's and O's on a piece of paper, while pretending to listen religiously to the message.

That evening we had a little surprise in store for us. When we arrived at the door of the church, one of the ushers led us right up to the front row. When we tried to object and tell him that we preferred a back seat he said, «The back seats are for late-comers.» We were sorry we had come early. We were obliged to listen to every word the evangelist said.

I shall never forget that meeting, because that evening I found the Lord, or to be more Biblically correct the Lord found me, «For the Son of Man is come to seek and to save that which was lost.» (Luke 19:10)

> Oh, the love that sought me,
> Oh, the blood that bought me,
> Oh, the grace that brought me
> to the fold.
> Wondrous grace that brought me
> to the fold.

Like Paul, I too had been kicking against the pricks. I was deeply convicted of my sins and knew that one day I would have to answer the question, «What will you do with Jesus, which is called the Christ?» I was not sure how I would answer that question.

I was afraid to die, and the coming of the Lord—often discussed at home—was a subject which filled me with terror. That evening Jock Troupe spoke on the coming of Christ! I was so convicted of my sins and so anxious to be saved that I could scarcely wait for the preaching to end in order to make a public decision for Christ. I knew I was going to give my answer that evening, and it was going to be positive. I was going to accept Jesus as my Savior and Lord.

However, when the evangelist made the appeal a great struggle was raging in my heart. I was very conscious of my brother's presence beside me. I turned to him and said, «Fred, would you like to accept Jesus with me tonight?» He said, «No.» Then I remembered the fellows with whom I worked and I thought, «How could I ever live a Christian life in that ungodly place?» I didn't wish to be a hypocrite, and I knew that my decision to accept Christ and live for Him would be for real.

I realized later that Jock Troupe was also aware of my struggle. I suddenly heard him say these words, «I believe there is a young fellow, tonight, in my meeting and you want to accept Christ as your Savior, but you are afraid to make that decision because you are afraid of your companions, your workmates, or your brother laughing at you. Let me warn you that your friends can laugh you into hell, but they can never laugh you out again. The Bible says, 'So then everyone of us shall give an account of *himself* to God.' (Romans 14:12) Whom are you going to choose tonight; your companions or Christ?»

My hand was raised high and I said in an audible voice, «Sir, I will accept Christ.» And I passed from death unto life. «Verily, verily I say unto you, He that heareth my word, and believeth on him that sent me, hath everlasting life, and shall not come into condemnation; but is passed from death unto life.» (John 5:24) That evening I heard Christ speaking to me through Jock Troupe. I heard His voice. I believed and I experienced a spiritual resurrection. Hallelujah!

When I got home that evening and told Mother that I had accepted Christ as my Savior, she said to me, «Robert, this is just the beginning; there is something more you must do; give your life entirely to God and ask Him to call you into His service.»

As I lay in bed that night I thought long and seriously about her words. Then it dawned upon me that she must have been praying this for me for a long time, even before I knew the Lord. I later learned that this was so.

Our family was as poor as most working-class families struggling in the depression years of the early thirties. We were a large family, and my father, a shipyard worker, was often unemployed. How my mother ever raised us as well as she did must have been due to a lot of faith and much hard work. Fortunately for all of us, she demonstrated both.

Mother had not always been a Christian, and only met the Lord when she was past forty. Two of my older sisters had already accepted Christ and were praying daily for her salvation. When she did come to Christ it was as if a spiritual revolution had taken place in our home. During the next several years one after another of her children came to know Christ as their Savior. Each was immediately given a missionary box to contribute to missions, and encouraged to read missionary biographies and attend missionary meetings and conventions.

When God began to prosper us so that we had a «prophet's chamber», it was more often occupied by missionaries than by any other class of Christian worker. Scores of missionaries from all over the world stayed with us when they came to Belfast. So it was comparatively easy for us children to hear God's call to foreign missionary service, because we were constantly exposed to the need of missions.

I believe my mother had truly learned to obey Christ's commandment to His disciples, «Pray ye therefore the Lord of the harvest, that he will send forth laborers into his harvest.» (Matthew 9:38) She not only faithfully prayed that prayer, but sought to answer it by giving half of her family as laborers for the harvest. Four of my sisters and I eventually went to Africa as missionaries.

I had several experiences during my teenage years that left deep impressions upon me. First of all, I realized that foreign missionary service begins at home, «in Jerusalem», then into Judea and Samaria and finally to the uttermost part of the earth. (Acts 1:8)

My Jerusalem was a butcher's store where I worked for an ungodly, dishonest man, whose five employees were not any more honest than he. When they learned that I had become a Christian, I became the butt of their filthy stories and ridicule. When I decided to wear a red button with the words *Jesus Saves* on the lapel of my jacket, my boss told me, «Take that daft thing off your jacket or leave this shop; there will be no Bible-thumpers working for me.»

Work was scarce and I had been delighted to find this job, but if I couldn't witness for Christ, then I would have to quit. I put on my jacket and started towards the door, but my employer stopped me and said, «Never mind, stay on your job, but just don't try to convert me or anyone else in this store.» I thought he might not fire me as I was doing a man's work for a boy's wages.

One of my workmates did become a Christian, and before I left to go to Bible college I had the opportunity every day to witness to the scores of customers I attended; my boss pretended not to notice. In fact, several years later when I left to go to college, he begged me to stay on and promised to give me a raise in my salary. As far as I know he never accepted Christ and died in unbelief.

Another teenage experience which left a deep impression upon me was the definite missionary call that I felt to serve the Lord in Africa. Several months after my conversion, I attended the annual *Faith Mission* convention in Bangor, Northern Ireland. The missionary meeting on Easter Tuesday afternoon was

14

always considered to be the highlight of the weekend convention. It was always attended by hundreds of young people from all over Ireland. That particular Easter Tuesday was no exception, and the atmosphere seemed charged with the presence of the Lord.

As the missionaries, one after another, presented the needs of the various foreign mission fields, I felt a great urge to confess publicly what I had already felt for months, that God wanted me to serve Him on a foreign mission field. I still recall with great joy the deep peace that flooded my heart as I wended my way to the front of the church with scores of others, to confess my willingness to serve the Lord anywhere He wanted me to go. It was a very definite decision I made that day. I returned to my home in Belfast with a strong sense of commission from the Lord.

About a year later, I attended a missionary prayer meeting in the home of an aunt who was also planning to go to the mission field. The speaker that evening was a young woman who was soon leaving for missionary work in Japan. Half a dozen of the young people present had already committed their lives for missionary service, and it was to them that she addressed her remarks.

«Some of you», she said, «feel called to serve the Lord on the foreign field. May I impress upon you the need not only to believe that you *feel* called to serve Christ overseas, but to *be sure* that he has given you a promise from His Word upon which you can place your 'spiritual feet', so that in the days of doubt and uncertainty, you can go back to God's Word and claim His promise for you.» Then she added, «And if God speaks to you in this manner, His Word will stand out like letters of gold.»

When I got home that evening I was a little bit troubled about my missionary call. I had to confess that God had certainly never spoken to me in that manner from His Word. I had seen no passage in the Bible stand out like «letters of gold». But I did appreciate her earnestness, and I knew that I could not go overseas simply because of some emotional experience. Yes, I felt I would need a confirmation of some kind from God's Word to assure me that the call I had felt deep down in my soul was from God.

When the rest of the family had gone to bed, I slipped down into the kitchen, which was the warmest room in the house. It was winter and the house was very cold. I got down on my knees and placed my Bible on a chair, and prayed very simply that God would speak to me in the way that young lady had indicated.

I don't know how long I stayed on my knees, and I don't recall how much of the Bible I read that night before I found the promise I was looking for. I remember I searched all the well known and often used missionary passages of the Bible in both Old and New Testaments. «Whom shall I send, and who will go for us? ...Here am I; send me.» (Isaiah 6:8) «As the Father hath sent me, even so send I you.» (John 20:21) «Go ye into all the world, and preach the gospel to every creature.» (Mark 16:15) «Come over into Macedonia, and help us.» (Acts 16:9) «Ye shall be witnesses unto me in Jerusalem, and in Judea, and Samaria, and to the uttermost part of the earth.» (Acts 1:8)

I read them all, but somehow none of them seemed to speak to me with conviction. Then almost in a spirit of desperation I prayed to the Lord a simple prayer. «Lord,» I prayed, «if You are calling me to the foreign mission field, speak to me clearly in the *present tense*. Assure me at this moment that You *are calling me.*»

After praying that prayer my Bible seemed to

open by itself at the First Epistle of Paul to the Thessalonians. My first reaction when I looked at this passage was, «Oh, there is nothing about a missionary call in this Epistle; it is concerned mostly with the coming of Christ.» However, I began to read at the first verse of chapter 1 and read through the whole Epistle. Imagine my excitement when I came to chapter five and verse twenty-four. Fortunately, I had not yet studied in a Bible College or Theological Seminary, so I knew nothing of contextual interpretation. I did not realize at that time that the words of verse twenty-four are closely linked with Paul's prayer for the Thessalonians in verse twenty-three, which speaks of entire sanctification. I simply read the words of verse twenty-four, and I must confess I read them in the light of what I had just prayed a few moments before, «Lord, if you are calling me, speak to me in the *present tense*.» I read, «Faithful is he that *calleth* (present tense) you, who also will do it.» I remember closing my Bible and praying again, «Lord, I will never doubt again that You want me to serve You on the foreign field.» And I really can't remember ever doubting His call after that.

> I heard His call, «Come follow»,
> That was all.
> Earth's joys grew dim, my soul
> went after Him.
> I rose and followed; that was all.
> Will you not follow if you hear His call?

It was the privilege of teenagers living in Northern Ireland in the thirties to grow up in what was almost a missionary revival. Bible schools all over Britain, for the most part, were filled with prospective missionary candidates.

In the church of which we were members, even though the minister was not particularly sympathetic with the missionary enthusiasm expressed by the young people of his church, twenty of them left for foreign missionary service, including several members of my own family.

The Christian Endeavour, sponsored by the young people, was the center of Christian activity and witness. Each summer at the beginning of June, the whole group took to the streets for open-air gospel meetings. The district where we lived was systematically covered, street by street, with gospel tracts placed in each home while the open-air meeting was in progress. By the end of the summer we had conducted meetings in every street, and spoken to hundreds about Christ on their doorsteps.

Sunday mornings saw many of us engaged in what was called Floating Endeavour. This we did before going to a Sunday morning worship service. The purpose of Floating Endeavour was to witness to the hundreds of seamen on ships in the Belfast docks. Some found Christ through this witness.

Every Saturday evening, winter and summer, a number of the Christian Endeavour members also held an open-air meeting between two pubs (taverns). At 10 p.m. everyone in the pubs had to leave because of the alcoholic licensing laws. Sometimes the customers were forcibly thrown out onto the street by the barmen, where they joined the open-air ring. At times it was difficult to restrain these drunk men from taking over the meeting and running it their way! But several were converted, including one of the barmen. This barman publicly confessed Christ at the ring and there and then quit his job. Later he found a better job where he did not have to compromise his testimony by selling liquor. For me, all of this Christian activity and witness was a wonderful preparation for Bible College, and later for the mission field.

Another privilege for which I shall always be grateful to the Lord, was the fact that I lived in a family where tithing was practised as the normal way of Christian living. As our family grew, material as well as accomodation needs became greater. The Lord led my mother and older sisters to start a little grocery business; later she specialized in children's clothing. My Mother's philosophy was that parents will buy clothes for their children much quicker than they would for themselves.

From the very beginning tithing was practised and the business grew. Soon we moved out of the small house in which we were living, to a larger dwelling on one of the main roads of the city. Part of this dwelling was converted into a clothing store. The Lord continued to prosper sales, and when a large butcher's store became vacant in a better business locality, the family took it over and promptly converted it into a clothing store.

The new shop was also dedicated to the Lord, and the first sale was promised to go to a Jewish mission. A few minutes after Mother opened the door, a small child entered and asked for a spool of thread. Mother was happy she didn't have the right color because the thread only cost a few cents. The next customer who entered made a substantial purchase; all of which was given to the Jewish mission.

It was a repeat story of the small shop. The more they sold, the more they gave, and business was booming. The store next door was failing because of a large cut-price chain store nearby. When the owner came one day and offered to sell the store with the «goodwill» (potential customers) Mother almost laughed, knowing his business was rapidly failing and it would be just as difficult for her to compete with the chain store as it had been for him.

But the shop next door had a fine dwelling above

it. Even though there was now enough accomodation for her own large family above the clothing store, the idea of having this extra accomodation where missionaries and others could be accomodated was very appealing to the whole family. So they took the step of faith and paid the neighbor for the shop and the non-existent goodwill! Two of my sisters took charge of this green grocery business, and, like the clothing store, it prospered and continued to do so until it was destroyed by German bombers in the Spring of 1943.

The war had come to Britain in the form of air raids by the German Luftwaffe. British cities and towns were being bombed systematically by the German bombers, and to add to the psychological fear and tension, Lord Haw-Haw (the name given to a British traitor who broadcast for the Germans all during the war, and was later hanged in London) would announce over the radio when and where the German bombers were going to strike; and they usually did—London, Birmingham, Coventry, Liverpool, and so on, and then Belfast.

In the two big air raids on the city of Belfast on Easter 1943, a land mine was parachuted which exploded about 100 feet above the ground not far from the shops. The tall spire of a neighboring Presbyterian church fell on the row of shops and the large police barracks at the end of the row. The shops and half of the police barracks were completely demolished, and several policemen were killed. Mother and one sister, and my younger brother James who was home on leave from the army, were sheltering underneath the stairs as the house had no basement or shelter from the bombs. The front part of the building collapsed, and it took two hours to dig them out from under the debris. Miraculously, none of them was killed or even injured. Their rescuers said over and over, «This is a miracle.»

Later Mother wrote to us in Africa telling us about this experience, and that they had lost everything they possessed. In her letter she quoted from the book of Job where the patriarch expressed his faith in similar circumstances: «The LORD gave, and the LORD hath taken away; blessed be the name of the LORD.» She continued to trust the Lord until she died eighteen months later. Three of the family were now in Africa: Janet in Liberia, and Emma and I in Spanish Guinea.

It was only when we returned to Ireland after the war that we learned from my sisters how triumphantly Mother had entered into the presence of the Lord, whispering the words of a hymn which she loved but was too weak to sing.

> Oh, this uttermost salvation,
> Tis a fountain full and free.
> Pure, exhaustless, ever flowing;
> Wondrous grace, it reaches me.

For me, this is how it all began.

CHAPTER 2

In The School Of Faith

A month after entering Bible College I celebrated my 19th birthday. Along with a dozen other Irish students, I entered the Bible College of Wales in Swansea, South Wales, to spend two years in what I have come to regard as «The School of Faith.»

I don't recall learning too much about the Bible, but it was there that I learned to trust the Lord in a way I had never known before. In many ways it was a very exciting experience which has stayed with me all my life. The way in which God answered prayer for the College needs, as well as my own personal needs, was a constant source of amazement to me. I believe I learned something of the truth which the Psalmist expressed in Psalm 118:8, «It is better to trust in the LORD than to put confidence in man.»

The Reverend Mr. Rees Howells, converted Welsh miner and founder of the Bible College of Wales, shared in the revival that swept through his native land in 1904-1905. Before and during his missionary career in South Africa, God had put His hand in a special way upon Rees Howells, to demonstrate His faithfulness in answering what seemed impossible prayers.

While serving with the South African General Mission, Mr. Howells was invited to speak and minister on every station of the Mission. Wherever he preached, the Holy Spirit used him in an unusual way to lead hundreds of Africans to Christ, and bring revival blessings to the churches.

It was during that time that God laid upon his heart the desire to found a Bible college, where some of the Spirit-taught principles he had learned and practised in his own ministry could be shared with young people, especially those who felt called to foreign missionary endeavor.

The story of Rees Howells' life and ministry is told in *Rees Howells - Intercessor,* by Norman Grubb. It is a thrilling story. Most of its contents we heard from the lips of Rees Howells himself. I shall always remember him as a mighty man of prayer, full of faith and full of the Holy Spirit. His life has been an inspiration to me during the years of my missionary career. I am grateful that he encouraged me to enter «The School of Faith.»

When the LORD spoke to Abraham in Genesis 18:14 and asked him, «Is anything too hard for the LORD?», the obvious answer was, «No, nothing is too hard for God.» He is the omnipotent God; He is the One with whom all things are possible. «With God all things are possible.» (Luke 1:37)

Many times Mr. Howells would say, «Yes, God can do all things, impossible things, but can He do them *through you*? This is the test of faith; you cannot trust God for big things until you have learned to trust Him for little things. Faith like grace must grow. Are you weak? Do you believe He can make you strong? Are you timid? Do you believe He can make you brave? Do you have a financial need? Can you trust Him to meet that need? Are you fearful? Can you trust Him to fill your heart with His peace?»

«The just shall live by faith.» (Romans 1:17) «We walk by faith, not by sight.» (II Corinthians 5:7) This was the teaching we heard day after day, and saw put into practice before our eyes. But how does it all become personal to me? Can I really trust the Lord in all these areas of need?

As I searched my heart those early days in «The School of Faith», I began to ask myself certain questions which I knew I was going to have to answer sooner of later. I also knew that the answer to those questions would influence my Christian way of living, and become part of my Christian philosophy. Was this the kind of life the Lord was leading me to live? Can I honestly trust God in all these areas of need?

I was convinced that the Lord had led me to the Bible College of Wales for my missionary preparation; of that I had no doubt whatsoever. I knew I gave mental assent to the teaching of the life of faith that I heard day after day. But there was always a lurking suspicion deep down in my heart that I was not really willing to put God to the test. In order to do this, rightly or wrongly, I made a certain decision. First of all, I would never make my needs known, and secondly, I would take no money from my family. I did not make this decision without much thought and prayer. I knew my family was more than willing to help me with my college expenses. I also realized that my action and attitude might be misunderstood by them and grievously hurt them.

War clouds were already appearing on the horizon. The year was 1935, and Italy had invaded Ethiopia. For three weeks the college suspended all work and studies, and we all spent the time in prayer and fasting. No food was served until six o'clock in the evening, and a light supper was served at 10 p.m. We prayed all day long and late into the night that God would overthrow the Italian forces and give deliverance to the hopelessly outnumbered and militarily unprepared Ethiopians. It seemed an impossibility. But those prayers were answered at the end of the 1939-1945 war, when the Ethiopian Emperor, Haile Selassie, returned victoriously to his homeland and people once more.

What if war should come and I should find myself on a foreign mission field, cut off from family and supplies? Could I trust God in those circumstances? The obvious answer was yes, but could I trust Him *now* to meet my needs in the present circumstances in which I found myself in college? The answer, of course, had to be yes. So I made my decision to enter «The School of Faith» and put my confidence entirely in the Lord and not in man or family. It was a decision that I have never once regretted.

It is difficult after forty years to recall in detail the many answers to prayer during those two years, as well as in the immediate years that followed. There were times of testing. Sometimes for weeks I didn't have two cents to buy a stamp to write home, or the money to pay my fees when they became due. This often called for hours of prayer and waiting upon the Lord.

The College had an unwritten rule that if term fees were not paid before the holidays began, then the student was expected to remain in school and work; without pay. Once, I didn't get home for fifteen months. But as the last term of my two-year course came to an end, I could look back and say, «Hitherto hath the Lord helped us... Great is thy faithfulness.» All my bills were paid, and I left the college debt free.

In 1936 I was accepted as a candidate by the Worldwide Evangelization Crusade to serve in the Ivory Coast, West Africa. To find myself in the Crusade headquarters in London, sharing daily in the life of missionaries coming and going to all parts of the world, and learning more of the life of discipleship, made my call a more definite reality. London seemed a little nearer to Africa than Swansea.

However, I had not yet reached my twenty-first birthday, and it was obvious to me, as well as to the Crusade leaders, that it would be some time before I would leave England for Africa. Mr. Grubb, General Secretary of the Worldwide Evangelization Crusade, called me and another young candidate and suggested to us that he thought it would be a good idea for us to get some kind of medical training before going to the field. We had plenty of time to do this as we were too young to expect to go to the foreign field. «I believe it will make you a more effective missionary if you do,» he added.

My companion, Jack Cairns, also from Ireland, was planning to do pioneer work in India. I believed God was calling me to a similar work in West Africa.

It was suggested that we apply to the Missionary School of Medicine in London. We couldn't do otherwise than agree to go, believing that this was the Lord's will for us. We both received a scholarship from MSM and registered as students.

Mr. Grubb informed us that we could stay at the WEC headquarters as long as our beds were not needed by other candidates who might enter later.

We stayed at the Mission center for about a month, cycling sixteen miles daily to and from the Missionary School of Medicine. At times it was a harrowing experience, especially when it rained, and that autumn it seemed to rain every day, sometimes all day long. We often arrived at the school drenched to the skin and covered with mud from passing cars.

We were both slowly coming to the conclusion that we should find lodgings nearer the school. Our only reason for not moving was that we did not have any money. But our minds were made up for us when the Crusade Candidate Secretary told us that a contingent of new Canadian crusaders was expected shortly. They needed our beds and he asked us to be prepared to move at the end of that week. So once again the Lord was putting us back into «The School of Faith». During that week we hunted for a room and found one about a mile from the school. To confirm our going, the Lord provided us each with five pounds (about twenty dollars at that time), enough money to pay our room and food for three weeks. In pre-war Britain, with its colonial empire, living was extremely cheap. We could live comfortably for a dollar and a half a day for both of us! We did not have to worry about food and lodging for three weeks.

We were kept so busy with studies and practical work at the MSM, that the days and weeks slipped by so fast we were not aware that suddenly our money and provisions had come to an end. I shall never forget the morning we ate what was left in the larder, and looked at one another wondering where our next meal would come from. «Give us this day our daily bread» was not prayed in the mechanical fashion in which we had so often uttered those words in Sunday School and church. It was a stark reality.

I had come to know one of the MSM students better than the others, and we became close friends. That same morning that our food was exhausted I was talking with Ron when one of the doctors arrived to give his lecture. Ron turned to me and said, «Bob, would it upset your plans if I were to ask you for lunch and we could finish our conversation in the restaurant?» I just smiled and said, «Not in the least; I'll be delighted to accept your invitation.» I never did tell Ron that his invitation that morning was a direct answer to the prayer we had prayed, «Give us *this day* our daily bread.»

After lunch I returned to our lodging wondering what Jack had eaten, if at all, and how God was going to supply our immediate needs. In a day or two we would also have to pay our rent. From every point of view our financial situation was pretty grim. When I entered our room I didn't need to ask Jack what he had had for lunch. He had a grin that covered his face. He didn't look hungry! «Look what my grandmother has sent us,» he said. There was a large parcel on the table filled with all kinds of bought and homemade foods. She had mailed it from Bangor several days before, and it had arrived on the day we literally did not have a crumb in the cupboard. She had also sent a substantial gift, which provided our needs almost to the end of the first term of school. We shared all things in common.

But it wasn't all easy. We had no heat in our room and had to wrap ourselves in blankets in order to study with some degree of comfort. When the cold became unbearable after two or three hours of study, we ran for a mile around the London zoo, and got back to our room warm and jumped into bed. We jogged in London every night that winter before jogging had ever been heard of.

All our cooking was done on a single gas ring,

and we became experts at making hot meals on this little ring. I smile sometimes at the kind of menus we invented, but most of them were eatable, and some of them extremely good. To this day I still enjoy cooking. We also appreciated the lessons we learned from one another as we were very different in our personalities.

At the end of the year, Jack and I passed all the exams and each won a prize besides receiving the MSM diploma. We left the Missionary School of Medicine with the feeling that we would not again see any of the fellows and girls we had studied with during those months. I have only met one of them since graduation in 1937.

Jack and I became part of the WEC family again, and it seemed like we had never been away. Africa was getting closer all the time. I began to think, «Well, I have to spend another six months at the Crusade headquarters» (the average time a candidate spent there), in order to become thoroughly acquainted with the Principles and Practices of the Crusade, or the P's and P's, as they were commonly called.

I also knew that I would have to spend several months to a year in France, in order to learn the language before going to the Ivory Coast. Patience has never been one of my virtues. I did not know that it would be three years before I would finally leave England for Africa.

At the time I was an accepted candidate, the WEC had an unwritten rule about candidates going to French-speaking countries. The Crusade only permitted six at a time to study in France. All were given an allowance out of the general fund. However, if a candidate wished to go at his own expense, he could do so.

It was January 1939, and there were six candidates ahead of me, including my sister, Janet. Theoretically, unless I could find the money, I would have to wait another nine months before I could go to France. I often wondered who was responsible for deciding on this arbitrary number, because it seemed logical to me—after some of my own experiences of trusting God—that he could provide for sixteen, or sixty for that matter, as well as six. I began to pray earnestly that God would provide enough funds to enable me to spend at least six months in France. He was to answer that prayer in the most unexpected way.

Miss Pavey was an elderly lady who lived alone in a small cottage about fifty miles from London. She was a great prayer-warrior and loved the WEC and everyone connected with it. Often she invited candidates to spend a weekend in her humble home, just to give them a break from the close community life they lived at the Crusade headquarters. She did not have much of this world's goods, but what she had she shared with others to the point of extreme sacrifice, often going without the necessities of life in order to support missionaries.

I did not know her personally. The first time I saw her at headquarters she was walking around in a pair of shoes that badly needed repair. At the Bible College of Wales, one of the students who was a cobbler by trade had taught me how to repair shoes. Every time I saw Miss Pavey that weekend I was tempted to ask her if I could repair her shoes, but I refrained from doing so, not wishing to embarrass her. Finally, I said to Janet, «Why don't you ask Miss Pavey, discreetly, if she would like one of the fellows to mend her shoes.» Miss Pavey was delighted, and in no time at all I had put soles and heels on them. After she left I thought no more about her.

A week later, however, I received a short thank-you note from Miss Pavey with a gift enclosed, sufficient to pay my expenses in France for four months. She could easily have bought herself not only one pair of shoes, but several, but she preferred to use the money to help prepare a future missionary for service in Africa.

That money was sacred to me. I felt somewhat like David when his three brave men brought him a drink from the well of Bethlehem, risking their lives to do so, and David, instead of drinking the water, poured it out unto the Lord as an act of worship. «Shall I render unto the Lord that which cost me nothing?» he said in another place, after God had shown him mercy and grace.

One lesson I did learn from Miss Pavey's sacrificial gift was that God will hold me responsible for my stewardship of money given to me by the Lord's people. The Lord has given us thousands of dollars since that time for our own ministry and the ministry of others. Faith, like grace, does grow as it is exercised for the glory of God.

On February 1, 1939, along with the six other WEC candidates, I crossed over to France. All of us lived in a small French Bible Institute in Nogent, in the suburbs of Paris. It was an exciting experience to find oneself in a new culture, and learning a new language for the first time. The eight months I spent there were among the happiest of my life.

Again the Lord permitted me to have certain experiences during that period of language study which were later to play an important role in my returning to France and spending twenty-three years of missionary service in that country. As in London, so in Paris, our finances ran out, and once again we proved that God can provide a table in the wilderness.

At the end of six months I had acquired a working knowledge of French, and could express myself fairly well. I enrolled as a student at *The Alliance Francaise* with the hope of obtaining the *Diplome de la Langue Francaise,* which would permit me to teach French, officially, in any French colony or American college. I felt very strongly, for reasons I could not explain at that time, that it was the Lord's will for me to obtain this diploma. It was also presumptuous on my part, as the majority of the advanced language students in the Alliance Francaise had been studying for a year or more to get this diploma.

I moved out of the *Institut Biblique de Nogent* into a Home for Young Men, sponsored by the Salvation Army. It was the cheapest lodging one could find in Paris. The rooms were clean, and the food palatable. I was joined there by Aubrey Brown, an Australian WECer, who had arrived in Paris to study French in order to go to Zaire. He and I shared a room to save money, but two weeks after he arrived our money ran out. It was London all over again.

We searched through our personal effects to see if we could sell something to some of the fellows in the Home, but the only thing that looked worth selling was a beautiful silk bathrobe that Aubrey had purchased in Alexandria on the way to England. But neither of us was a good salesman, and after trying in the Home and on the streets of Paris, we returned to the Home hungry and discouraged, wondering how the Lord was going to supply our needs. There was no one, humanly speaking, who could help us.

As soon as we entered the Home we made a beeline for the mail boxes, and sure enough there was a letter for me from a missionary friend in Africa. My first reaction, when I saw who it was from, was not too positive. I opened the envelope and found a French postal order inside. When I read the letter, I discovered that the money was for the purchase of

33

a missionary biography published in France, that this person was anxious to buy. She wanted me to buy it and send it to her. However, she wrote a P.S. at the bottom of her letter, saying, «If you can't find the book, don't worry; just keep the money as a gift.»

I read the letter to Aubrey and said to him, «How diligently should we look for this book?» Aubrey laughed and said, «Well, Bob, there are only two bookstores in this district; let's try to see if we can find the book.» We did, and to our great relief we learned that the book was out of print! The postal order was enough to pay our modest rent and meals for a few days.

I said I *hoped* to obtain the *Diplome de la Langue Francaise*. I have reason for writing thus, because there was a ten dollar fee for the examination, and ten dollars was a small fortune to us at that time. So in spite of my presumption in believing I could pass the exam, because the Lord had endowed me with a good memory and I have never had too much difficulty learning languages, that ten dollar fee loomed large on the horizon of my hopes. But I kept studying, ten, twelve and sometimes fourteen hours a day, practically memorizing the textbook we were using. The day of the exam arrived, and I still didn't have the ten dollar fee. I remember going into school that morning, wondering why the Lord had not answered this prayer when I felt so sure it was His will for me to take the exam.

To this day, I don't know why I went into the office to ask the girl behind the desk whether it was too late to register for the exam. I was still hoping for a miracle. «Yes,» she answered, «it is. What is your name?» I told her and she said, «But, Sir, you have registered already and here is your card for the examination room.» I was flabergasted.

I said to her, «But, Madamoiselle, I have not paid for the exam.»

She checked the records and said, «Well, Sir, if *you* haven't paid for it, someone else has. Here is your card, and good luck for the examination.»

The exam was to begin in a few minutes so I rushed to the examination room, not depending on good luck, but confident that the Lord who had touched someone's heart to pay my fee, was the same Lord who would bring to my remembrance all that I had studied the past month. And He did. The exam was more or less based on the textbook I had practically memorized, and I answered most of the questions easily. Two days later when we took the oral exam, I was assigned to two professors who were quite pro-British, and certainly very lenient and generous with the marks they gave me. I got the diploma. Praise God!

It was a very wonderful and satisfying experience of trusting the Lord for this particular need. Years would pass before I would fully understand why I had worked so hard to receive this diploma, because I never did go to the Ivory Coast.

The other experience I had in France which was to play an important role in my going there later as a missionary, was the influence of Dr. Ruben Saillens, founder of the *Institut Biblique de Nogent.* Dr. Saillens was one of France's outstanding Christian leaders. As an evangelist and Bible teacher, *extraordinaire,* he was used of God to win souls and edify the Church of Christ, not only in his native land, but also in England, where he spoke at the Keswick convention, and in Holland, where he was often invited by the Dutch Queen to preach to her family and the palace household.

All the members of the Saillens family were as fluent in English as their father, and several of them successfully carried on his ministry at the *Nogent Bible Institute,* as well as in the *Paris Tabernacle Baptist Church,* which Dr. Saillens also established.

Doctor Saillens was a great anglophile. He was particularly interested in the group of British students studying French in his Bible school. On one occasion he invited us all to go with him on a tour of Paris. When we arrived at the top of Montmartre and looked out over the city (two-thirds of which can be seen from this vantage point), Dr. Saillens turned to us and said, «I'm grateful to God that He is leading you all to help in the evangelization of France's colonies in West Africa. But if for any reason you cannot go, or are forced to return to Europe, do not forget the spiritual need of la belle France.» Then, looking out over the city, and with a sweeping gesture of his arm, he said again, «*Voila jeunes gens, votre paroisse*»—there, young people, is your parish.

I was very weary when I finished studying at the Alliance Francaise, so it was with unusual pleasure that I accepted a job in Morges, Switzerland. I joined a team of five fellows in erecting the large Morges convention tent, and preparing the conference grounds for the summer meetings, and doing general maintenance work. The good, hard physical work was such a pleasant change from studying all day long. The weather, the good food, and the breathtaking beauty of Switzerland were all like a dream to me. I was completely ignorant and oblivious to the fact that war was imminent. It seemed so unreal and so amoral in the quiet neutrality of Switzerland. I had no radio, and hadn't read a newspaper in weeks, so I was quite unprepared for the shock we were to receive one morning in one of the meetings.

Many visitors had already left the conference center sooner than they had planned. But the bombshell dropped the morning that Dr. Rene Pache, chairman of the conference, arrived in his military uniform and announced, that because of the political situation between Germany and the Allies, and the imminent possibility that France and England were going to declare war against Germany—the German armies had already invaded Poland a few days previously—the conference committee had reluctantly decided to terminate the conference that morning. He wished us Godspeed and a safe return to our homes.

I was stunned, and my first reaction was, «If war does come, what about my missionary aspirations?» That question would be answered in ways undreamed of.

That same evening I managed to get the last train leaving for Paris before the Swiss military took over the railroads. It took all night for the train to reach Paris; stopping, it seemed, at every station. How people got on and off I do not know, because we were crushed in the compartments and corridors like sardines. I spent a sleepless night standing in the corridor, and was glad when the train pulled into Paris as dawn was breaking.

The streets were already filled at that early hour with people rushing hither and thither, and almost every Frenchman was in uniform. I immediately went out to Nogent to see if Janet and the other WEC candidates were still there, but the school was closed and everyone had left.

I then made my way to the British Embassy to see if it were wise, or possible, to stay on in France. I wanted so much to be able to spend at least six months in a French milieu to perfect my knowledge of French. But I also realized that this might not be possible, as I would very likely be conscripted into the British army and join my two brothers who were already enlisted.

When I reached the Embassy it was closed, and

a number of people were waiting to get in. After an hour or so the door opened and an official said to us, «Ladies and gentlemen, His Excellency the Ambassador has instructed me to tell you that if you have no official reason for remaining in France, please leave immediately. It may be difficult, if not impossible, to do so later.»

I went directly to St. Lazare railroad station and purchased a ticket to London via Dunkirk. By the time the train arrived in Dunkirk it was nearly midnight. There was just one ferry leaving for England, and it was rumored that it would be the last for several days. There must have been fifteen hundred people waiting to board the boat. I was among the last to press up the gangway, and when I got on board I discovered that it was standing-room only.

The boat didn't leave until 3 a.m., and I spent another sleepless night. When we arrived in Dover, and later in London, everyone was going about his or her business in a calm sort of way—so different from what I had witnessed in Paris the day before. But I did notice that almost everyone was carrying a gas mask slung over the shoulder, and there were air raid shelters everywhere. Yes, it surely looked like England was expecting war.

By this time the German armies had almost overrun all of Poland, and England, Poland's ally, must declare war on Germany at any moment.

I finally reached my destination outside London, where some friends had invited me to stay with them for a few days. It was five p.m. Saturday when I arrived at their home. I had been traveling since Thursday evening without sleeping, so after a quick bath and a meal, I went to bed and fell unconscious. I didn't waken until two p.m. on Sunday.

When I went down into the living room, the family looked at me and smiled. I asked them what was funny, and they replied, «You are.» Then they told me that Neville Chamberlin, the British Prime Minister, had declared that morning at 11 a.m. that England was at war with Germany. A few minutes after his announcement, the first of what was later to be thousands of air raid warnings, was sounded and scores of fighter planes from a nearby airfield had flown low over the house with tremendous noise, rattling windows and scaring everyone to death, and I had slept peacefully through it all!

But what about my call to Africa? Would I ever get there, or would I be caught up in the war effort which seemed to me to be inevitable? A promise I had found that night on my knees as a teenager, came back to me with renewed force and assurance, «Faithful is he that calleth you who also will do it.» I knew God would somehow do it for me, and He did. But before I would arrive in Africa, there were many more lessons to be learned in «The School of Faith.»

CHAPTER 3

Let The Dead Bury Their Dead

The day after war was declared I returned to the WEC headquarters in southeast London. About fifty missionaries and missionary candidates were present. The thought uppermost in everyone's mind was, «How is the war going to affect us all as missionaries? Shall we be able to obtain visas and get boat passages to the fields to which we are going? Will the government regard missionary work as important enough to exempt missionaries from military service?»

The first weeks of the war were a time of great heart searching and trying to find one's priorities and the will of God in all these matters. I had no doubt that God would reveal His will to us as individuals and as a Mission.

The «phony war», as it was called, dragged on in Europe until the spring of 1940. Apart from strict rationing of every commodity and blackouts, life was not too abnormal in wartime Britain. Then the German armies moved into Norway, Denmark, Holland, Belgium and France in that order. In a few weeks it was all over for those countries. It was a veritable blitzkrieg—lightning war—and they would remain under German occupation for four long years.

The last remnant of the British and French forces (about 340,000 men), retreated to England from Dunkirk. For several days they were ruthlessly bombarded on the beaches at Dunkirk by the German army and air force. Every available boat that was seaworthy was comandeered by the British Royal Navy and sent across the channel to participate in the greatest rescue mission in history. For days there was not a ripple upon the channel and the soldiers crossed over to England in every kind of craft imaginable. Many of the men had to stand in the rowboats and lifeboats that were towed by a motorboat or larger vessel. The retreat was later described by war historians as «The Miracle of Dunkirk.» Mr. Winston Churchill, however, quickly reminded the nation that wars were not won by successful retreats.

Another French-speaking WECer and I were invited by a pastor in Eastbourne, on the south coast of England, to spend a few weeks with him in order to witness to the hundreds of French soldiers who were billeted in Eastbourne. Scores among them had been seriously wounded and were in the hospital. Day after day as we talked with these *poilus,* we came to believe that most of them had lost all hope of an allied victory. For them *la guerre était finie; tout était perdu*—the war was finished; all was lost. Many of them expected and wished to be repatriated to their families in France. We began to realize as never before how difficult it would be for anyone to leave England except for military service.

When we returned to London rumors were flying around that the government was going to call up every able-bodied man and woman into the war effort. In Eastbourne we had seen middle-aged men and older in the Home Guard, parading and doing maneuvers without uniforms or firearms. The allied armies had retreated so fast from France that many of the soldiers did not even bring back their rifles. It was apparent to all that the war was on England's doorstep.

The German armies were massing on the other side of the English Channel. Goering's air force had already begun what later came to be known as the Battle of Britain. Because of the situation, I must confess that I did wonder if we would ever be permitted to leave the country, and the possibility of going to Africa was receding more and more.

Mr. Grubb's spiritual leadership of the Worldwide Evangelization Crusade was always deeply appreciated by every Crusader, but especially during those months of uncertainty. His strong faith and determination to keep true to the Crusade's motto—the evangelization of the world—never wavered. At times I felt I was back again in Swansea, as the same truths taught by Mr. Howells were being reiterated day after day by Mr. Grubb. I slowly began to believe, and to believe firmly, that war or no war, God was going to permit me to go to Africa.

However, as the rumors of an imminent call-up became more persistent, three of us fellows decided that if we should be called up, we would try to serve in a non-combattant organization. Several such organizations existed, whose employees were recognized as contributing to the war effort.

We decided to try two of them: The Peace Pledge Union and the Quakers. The Peace Pledge Union, we discovered, was a cover-up for Sir Oswald Mosley's fascist organization, later outlawed by the British government. The Quakers were interested in enrolling us in one of their ambulance units because of our paramedical training received at the Missionary School of Medicine. However, they wanted to send us to China and none of the three of us wished to go to that particular part of the world.

When we got out on the street we looked at one another and I said to my companions, «Well, fellows, where do we go from here?»

One of them answered and said, «Back to our room at headquarters to ask the Lord where He wants us to go. We need His direction in our lives.»

That evening the three of us decided to fast and pray in our rooms and seek to know God's definite will for our immediate future. That same morning in prayers, Mr. Grubb had said something that really challenged me. He said, «Some of you men may be called to serve in the armed forces, and if you do, then live like Christian crusaders. But if God permits you to go to your field of service, whatever that might be, then live like true soldiers of Jesus Christ.» Good advice for any prospective missionary.

In my room I prayed, «Lord, here I am; if I have to go into the army, I'll live like a missionary; if I go to the mission field of Africa, I'll live like a soldier. Please show me Your will in this; what must I do?»

I began to read Luke's Gospel, chapter 9, and my eyes were riveted on verses 60 and 62. I read the words, «Jesus said unto him, Let the dead bury their own dead, but you go and proclaim the kingdom of

God… no one who puts his hand to the plough and looks back is fit for the kingdom of God.» (N.I.V.)

If God had spoken those words to me audibly, they could not have been any more real, «Let the dead bury their own dead…» This was to become literally true in the city of London, where thousands were killed in the air raids that started about that time and continued more or less for the duration of the war.

My faith was once again greatly strengthened after reading this passage in Luke. Almost immediately afterwards the Lord confirmed and tested my faith. This seems to be a divine principle in the life of faith. He gives us assurance followed by testing.

The assurance came in the form of a government announcement that all ministers and missionaries accepted by bona fide missions would be exempted from military service or any other aspect of the war effort. To their credit, the British government recognized the need for spiritual as well as physical efforts if the war was to be won.

The testing came in the form of a phone call from Belfast to say that Mother was seriously ill in the hospital. The doctors didn't give much hope for her recovery. Could we come home before she died?

The difficulty about leaving England at that particular time was that anyone who left the country could not return without special permission from the government. This was especially true for those returning from or living in Northern Ireland.

The Republic of Ireland (Eire) remained neutral throughout the war. The German Embassy still functioned in Dublin. It was comparatively easy for anyone from the Republic to go north to Belfast and then slip across to England. Therefore, any person crossing to Britain from Ireland was automatically suspect.

Special permission would be needed for Janet and me to return to England if we left. We were informed, officially, that this would not be easily given, probably refused. So if we went to Belfast, we would undoubtedly have to stay there for the duration of the war. What to do? It was an agonizing decision to make.

Janet and I went to see Mr. Grubb to ask him for his advice. The advice he gave us was very simple and very direct. «Robert and Janet», he said, «If you were soldiers at the front line of battle and heard that your mother was dying, you wouldn't be able to leave. I know your Mother well, and I do not believe for a moment that she would want you to see her before she dies, if she thought that your going would prevent you from getting to Africa for several more years. Jesus exhorts us in His Word, 'Let the dead bury their own dead, but go you and proclaim the kingdom of God.' God has called you both to be crusaders in this Crusade; now He is giving you an opportunity to prove to Him that you can be true soldiers of Jesus Christ. You have asked me what you should do, should you go or not? My advice is simple; don't go.»

Mr. Grubb prayed with us and committed Mother to the Lord. She did not die but lived for three more years, although Janet and I never saw her again. But when she was well enough to write to us, she told us how thankful she was that we had made the decision not to return to Belfast. My mother was also a true soldier of Jesus Christ!

This testing of our faith was very precious to us. It was not the first and would not be the last before we would arrive in Africa, but they were all certainly in God's plan for us. Peter, in his First Epistle, chapter 1:6, 7, expresses it thus: «In this you greatly rejoice, though now for a little while you have had to suffer grief in all kinds of trials. These have come so that your faith—of greater worth than gold, which perishes even though refined by fire—may be proved genuine and may result in praise, glory and honour when Jesus is revealed.» (N.I.V.)

Most of the summer of 1940 the war was fought over Britain, and London in particular was the target of Hitler's bombs. It was impossible sometimes to tell whether an air raid was on or off, they were so frequent. It seemed like the sirens blew all day long. Hundreds of Londoners slept in the deep underground railway stations.

Every evening, for weeks at a time, the German bombers would appear just before nightfall. They seemed always to follow the same route. The WEC headquarters was situated just a few miles from the big R.A.F. station at Croydon on the one side and the East docks of London on the other. So, much of the aerial fighting was done right above the WEC headquarters. We watched fascinated as the Royal Airforce Spitfires from Croydon would fly up to meet the German bombers and fighters as they approached the heart of London. Dogfights took place right above us and it was impossible to tell which fighters had been shot down until the news was broadcast later. England had her back to the wall.

If the retreat from Dunkirk had been hailed as a miracle, what about the Battle of Britain? No wonder Winston Churchill's famous statement concerning these young RAF pilots, who gave their lives for their country, became immortal, «Never in the history of human endeavor has so much been owed by so many to so few.»

I often thought as I watched these young men on both sides being shot down to their death, «If they can give their lives for their country, surely I can lay down mine, if need be, for Christ.» The motto of the Worldwide Evangelization Crusade is, «If Jesus Christ be God and died for me, then no sacrifice can be too great for me to make for Him.» (C.T. Studd)

There was no way we could know when we might leave England. The Mission had requested the government for exit visas for six of us to go to West Africa. All of us were headed for the Ivory Coast, but because England had no diplomatic relations with the Vichy government, it was impossible for us to obtain visas.

There were two options open to us. I was told by the WEC leaders that I could go to Spanish Guinea in Equatorial Africa and join my sister Emma, who was virtually working there alone. However, the problem of obtaining a visa from the Spanish government was just as difficult because the Franco government in Spain was not sympathetic to England, or any other of the Allies, for that matter. Spain was quite pro-German. So we were faced with all kinds of obstacles.

However, I told Mr. Grubb that I would be willing to go to Spanish Guinea, if it were possible to go there from a neutral West African country or a British colony. We had learned that there was a certain amount of freedom of passage between French Cameroon and Spanish Guinea, so if one could get to Cameroon, the problem of entering Spanish Guinea might be solved. In the hope of doing that I began to study Spanish. I did eventually go to Spanish Guinea, but certainly not the way I had anticipated. God's ways are not our ways, neither are His thoughts our thoughts. But God's way is perfect and He maketh my way perfect. (Psalm 18:30, 32)

The other option was for the whole party to go to the Republic of Liberia. Missionaries there were anxious to have more personnel and had already written to Mr. Grubb asking him if we six missionaries could be sent to reinforce the WEC work in Liberia. Visas to enter the country were comparatively easy to obtain; there were regular boat services from Liverpool to Monrovia and Buchanan. We were all willing to go and began to pray that God would make possible our departure from England.

There was absolutely no way of knowing when our exit permits would be granted because of the tight security measures at all British ports. Not even seamen ashore knew when their ship would leave until hours before its departure.

The only ray of hope we received about our exit permits was when the censorship department arranged an interview by one of their censors. This meant that we had to take all books, letters and documents for censorship. We were allowed to take only a small number of books as each one had to be carefully examined, as were all other documents, diplomas, notes, etc. The lady censor who examined my box asked me no questions until she examined my Bible, which was copiously marked with different colors. I spent nearly two hours trying to explain to her why I had marked certain passages with certain colors, and the meaning of the marginal notes I had made in my Bible. Her responsibility was to make sure that I was not taking some kind of code out of the country in my Bible! I was impressed how carefully she examined every piece of printed material. She was exposed at least to the doctrine of salvation which I explained to her from my Bible notes. She seemed woefully ignorant of anything spiritual.

Finally all my books and documents were sealed and the box could not be opened until it arrived in Liberia. Praise the Lord; it looked like we were at last really on our way to Africa. Our tickets had been purchased although we still didn't know the date of our departure. The years of hoping and waiting to go to Africa were fast coming to a close. My heart was dancing and I was praising God as I returned to WEC headquarters. It was September 5, 1940. A week later we left London for Liverpool and Liberia.

My last memory of London was leaving Euston Railroad Station. About forty friends from headquarters and one or two London churches had come to bid us farewell. Our party consisted of Bill and Edith Freeman from New Zealand, Alice Hausser from France, Juliette Voiral from Switzerland, my sister Janet and myself. As the train pulled out of Euston Station and headed out into the open country, we heard the unmistakeable wail of the air raid sirens. We were to hear them a couple of times more in Liverpool and then no more. When the war was over the British government forbade the use of sirens by the police or fire engines. Another form of «heehaw» warning was instituted instead. Everyone in wartime Britain had heard enough siren wails to last a lifetime.

We had the railway compartment to ourselves and spent a good part of the journey to Liverpool praising God for all that he had done for us. We were tremendously excited at the prospects of leaving England in a couple of days. The shipping company had told us that we would be given final instructions on Friday evening about boarding our ship.

The Lord had brought us thus far on our journey, removing the many obstacles that had beset our pathway. We were sure that He would bring us to our desired haven and the words of Psalm 107:28-31 were very real to us. «Then they cry unto the Lord in their trouble, and he bringeth them out of their distresses. He maketh the storm a calm, so that the waves thereof are still. Then are they glad because they be quiet; so he bringeth them to their desired haven. Oh, that men would praise the Lord for his goodness and his wonderful works to the children of men!» We were not yet at our desired haven, but we were confident the Lord would lead us there.

Our party stayed in Birkenhead a couple of nights at Emmanuel Bible College. On Friday afternoon Janet and I crossed over again to Liverpool to visit my father, who was temporarily working in the Liverpool shipyards. He was not a Christian and we wanted to talk to him about his spiritual need as well as say goodbye. We didn't know whether we would see him again. On the way back to Birkenhead, just as we boarded the ferry to cross the Mersy River, the air raid sirens began to wail. It was the first time the Liverpudians had heard them. It was the first German air raid on that city. It was 10 p.m. and dark, and Janet and I knew from our experience in London that the bombers would not arrive until about fifteen to twenty minutes after the warning. We had time to get back to the Bible College—we thought. But this time we were mistaken, because before the ferry reached Birkenhead, hundreds of incendiary bombs were already raining down on the docks and a number of fires were raging in different parts of the city.

My heart still beats fast at the memory of that race that Janet and I ran as we searched for an air raid shelter. There were always a number of these around the docks area, but in the darkness we couldn't locate any. So we ran as fast as we could to the nearest street and knocked frantically on a door. It was opened by an elderly couple who invited us immediately into their home. We discovered they were believers. They were comforted by our presence as we were by theirs. We were all horribly scared as the bombs continued to explode in the city. It wasn't much safer inside their little house than out on the street, but it felt safer.

An hour or so later the all-clear was sounded and we finally arrived at the College around midnight, much to the relief of our colleagues who were anxiously waiting our safe arrival. None of them had gone to bed. None of us will easily forget that last night in England.

As I am typing this account of that air raid, the siren is wailing from the roof of a fire station close by, and it reminds me so forcefully of that last air raid that we experienced in England!

On Saturday morning the shipping company phoned to tell us where to contact a small ferry that would take us out to our ship, anchored in the Mersy River about a mile from Birkenhead. This was it. We were finally leaving England. There were three other passengers besides ourselves and several seamen on the ferry when we arrived. We passed scores of ships in the river and finally stopped alongside of a 4,000 ton cargo ship called the *M.V. SANGARA*. The gangway was lowered and with mixed feelings we boarded her. The ship was brand new and had just returned from her maiden voyage to West Africa. Each of us was given a spacious cabin. The cabin steward told us that we would be eating at the captain's table during the voyage.

«There's another thing you need to know,» he added. «When you retire at night, leave your passport handy, and your important personal papers and your valuables, as well as whatever clothes you might need for a quick departure from the ship, in case it should be torpedoed.» Then he continued with a broad grin, «But I don't suppose anything like that could happen to us with so many missionaries on board; you'll be good insurance for the safety of the *SANGARA*.» Actually the *SANGARA* was sunk by a German submarine two days after we disembarked in Liberia. We learned this several years later. The

Captain, to whom we witnessed often and who was a kind and gentle person, was the only one apparently who was lost with the ship. It was torpedoed on a still, calm tropical night as it rode at anchor off an African port in Ghana.

We were just getting ready to go to our first meal when the air raid sirens began to wail. It was a bright sunny afternoon. We thought, «Surely this must be a false alarm because the German bombers usually appear after dark, and especially this far north a daylight raid is unlikely.» But we were mistaken for the second time. When everybody went out on deck for a better view there they were; six Junkers flying in formation like Canadian geese. For the next ten minutes scores of anti-aircraft guns shot at them, not only on land but from several warships anchored in the Mersy River. Two of the planes were shot down. That was our last glimpse of the war as it was being fought over Britain.

That night we left Liverpool accompanied by about thirty other ships and sailed for a secret rendezvous in northwest Scotland. When we woke up on Sunday morning we discovered that we were now part of a huge convoy that stretched for miles. I shall never forget the sight of that tremendous convoy as we left the shores of Scotland, surrounded by warships and protected by planes overhead. It was thus we left the shores of Britain and headed west across the Atlantic.

The Freemans suggested that we all go down to their cabin and commit our journey to the Lord. Bill opened his Bible and read from Isaiah 55:12, «You will go out *in joy* and be led forth *in peace*.» What a marvelous promise with which to begin our journey to Africa! These words from Scripture expressed perfectly our feelings at that moment. The joy and the peace of the Lord flooded our souls.

We stayed in convoy four or five days, zig-zagging all the time. It was reassuring to watch the warships sailing up and down each side of the convoy, as well as in front and behind. On the fifth day, however, we encountered rough weather with gale force winds that slowed up the convoy. The following day we woke up to find that our ship was all alone in the middle of the Atlantic. We felt very vulnerable to submarines.

The *SANGARA* had two Royal Navy sailors on board to man the gun at the stern of the ship. All cargo ships were armed in this way. One day the sailors practised firing at a target they had thrown overboard about a quarter of a mile astern. We were down in our cabins at the time the first shell exploded. It sounded for all the world like the ship had been struck by a torpedo. I remember grabbing my passport out of the drawer and rushing up to the main deck, trying to remember what lifeboat station I was supposed to go to, and thanking God that the ship had been torpedoed in the daytime and not at night. What a tremendous relief to learn that it was only gunnery practice, and not a submarine attack!

We watched the gunners firing for awhile but their shots never seemed to get too close to the target, from what we were told by one of the passengers who was watching through powerful binoculars. I couldn't help thinking again of what the Psalmist wrote, «It is better to trust in the Lord than to put confidence in man.»

Three weeks later we landed off the coast of Liberia, after stopping briefly in Freetown, Sierra Leone. When the ship dropped anchor about a mile off shore at Lower Buchanan we got our first good look at the country where we all thought we were going to spend the rest of our lives. It looked exactly like what I had always visualized that part of Africa might be. There were clusters of houses of the Kru tribe, situated among coconut plams and a large group of people assembled on the beach waiting for our arrival.

Buchanan, where we landed, was not a big town but it did have the distinction of having ships call there because of several large trading stores in the area. There is now a regular port at Buchanan, which was built later to handle the iron ore, now exported in great quantities.

For some time I had become accustomed to the idea that it would be just as profitable and needful to serve the Lord in Liberia as in any other part of West Africa. After all, just a small stream separated Liberia from the Ivory Coast. Of the tribes living along the frontier, part lived in Liberia while the other part lived in Ivory Coast. The only difference was that English is the official language of Liberia, while French is recognized as the official language of Ivory Coast.

It took an hour or more for four large surf-boats, about twenty feet long, to reach the *SANGARA*. Our luggage and some cargo were hoisted into these and we followed, sitting among boxes and trying to avoid being hit by the rowers. We had about forty boxes and trunks among the six of us. We had been advised to bring all kinds of stuff with us, enough to last for five years. I never used a third of what I took to Africa and sold or gave it away.

An hour later we finally landed on the beach and were welcomed by Mr. and Mrs. Horace Davey, Canadian leaders of Liberian Inland Mission, as WEC is known in Liberia. Emma Wisser, the Gaypeter station leader, and Jack Lenny, with whom I had studied at the Bible College of Wales, were also there to meet us. They had brought fifty to sixty porters to carry our luggage into the interior.

It was all very exciting. That night as I lay for

the first time under a mosquito net, listening to the tropical night sounds and the beating of native drums in a nearby village, my heart was filled with gratitude and praise to God for all the way that He had led me from the time I had written as an eight-year old boy, «Some day I shall follow in the footsteps of David Livingstone.» Well, I might not be literally following his footsteps, but at least I was in Africa and profoundly happy that the Lord was going to permit me to preach the kingdom of God there— something for which I had worked and prayed about for many years.

> Let the dead bury their own dead
> but you go and proclaim the kingdom
> of God.
> Faithful is he that calleth you who
> also will do it.

HALLELUJAH!

CHAPTER 4

Pioneering In Liberia

Liberia is the oldest black republic in Africa. It is a coastal state, situated between Sierra Leone and the Ivory Coast. Its coastline runs for about three hundred and fifty miles along the bulge of the African continent. The country stretches inland for some two hundred miles.

Liberia has a population of 1,600,000, ten per cent of which claim direct descent from the Americo-Liberians. The rest of the population is made up from the large tribes such as the Kpelle, Kru, Bassa, Mano, Gio and Grebe.

The establishment of Liberia as an independent country was brought about by the National Colonization Society founded in the USA in 1816 for the purpose of aiding American freed slaves to return to

Africa. Liberia declared its independence in 1824, and was recognized as such by France and England some years later. In 1862 the United States recognized Liberia's independence and from that time Liberia has maintained close identification and association with the USA to the extent of using American currency.

Politically, Liberia, until a few months ago when a military coup overthrew the government, has been one of Africa's most stable republics. There is complete religious liberty and foreign missions are encouraged and aided by the government, which permits missions and individual missionaries to import everything they need for their work, duty free. The Liberian government has always recognized the spiritual as well as the educational contribution that foreign missions have made to the national life. Radio ELWA (sponsored by the Sudan Interior Mission), situated near Monrovia, is Africa's best known Christian radio station, broadcasting the Word of God in forty different languages throughout the continent, reaching Arab and non-Muslim Africans alike.

In 1938 the Worldwide Evangelization Crusade sent its first pioneer missionaries to Liberia; six Canadians, one Englishman and two Irish fellows. The party divided into three groups, one working among the Bassa tribe near the coast, and the other two working among the Mano and Gio tribes in the interior. They had just established a foothold among these tribes when our party arrived to reinforce them.

The work was still very much in the pioneering stage, with missionary dwellings, simple school buildings and clinics in the course of erection on each station. Most of the interior of the country was still unmapped at that time, so the missionaries were also engaged in making rough maps, noting the density of the towns and villages and population. There was a great need of skilled workers: evangelists, teachers, nurses, builders and carpenters to help in every aspect of the work.

For example, there was only one practising physician in an area of several hundred square miles. He was German and an admirer of Adolf Hitler and the Nazi Party, so most of the missionaries were reluctant to consult him about their physical needs. The nearest dentist was in Monrovia, 100 miles distant, and this distance had to be covered on foot. Even the limited knowledge of medicine and dentistry such as we had received at the Missionary School of Medicine was of inestimable value. As one of the Christian doctors who lectured at the MSM often remarked, «Students, half a loaf is better than no loaf at all.» Many times I thanked the Lord for the training I had received at the Missionary School of Medicine, and others did too, who benefited from my limited medical and dental knowledge.

I was in the country only a week when an African woman came to me in great pain and begged me to extract her teeth. «All of them,» she said. Actually only two were bad and these I extracted without an anesthetic. They were to be the first of scores that I would extract in the next five years for blacks and whites in Liberia and Spanish Guinea.

During the first week we were obliged to stay in Buchanan, waiting for our mail which had come out on our ship but was not yet distributed by the local post office. Then, too, although we paid no customs duty, our baggage still had to be cleared by a customs officer. This was a mere formality, but a chance for him to expect a «dash»—a tip. We were soon to learn that the words «dash» and «wait small», meaning to wait a little while, are the words most often used and heard in conversations with Liberians, and especially among the tribes peoples. Liberia has been described by someone as «the land of wait small».

We also quickly learned that if a person cannot read or write, he or she is regarded as a «bushman» or a «bushwoman». I do not believe that this term is used in a derogatory manner, but simply to make a distinction between the educated and the illiterate.

However, we also observed that the so-called bushman is not by any means an ignorant person. On the contrary, he is often very intelligent, with a prodigious knowledge of the forest, its flora and fauna. His knowledge of bush medicine, i.e., the use of natural medicines extracted from plants, often astonished me.

Then, too, he is endowed with an amazing memory and can easily repeat the names of his forefathers back to fifteen generations or more. When it comes to learning languages, this is child's play for him, because he is a born mimic. This ability, coupled with his good memory and his easy facility to recognize the difference in tones (almost every West African language is tonal), enables him to become a linguist, par excellence. This is one gift the average African possesses that the foreign missionary envies.

We were not in the country long until we also recognized that the average bushman is quite a philosopher who wins most of the arguments with the missionary. In fact, it is hard to get the better of him in any given situation. I often wondered as I watched him work for the educated black or white, «Who is the real servant, he or they?»

I came to have the greatest respect for the African living in the bush. Many times as he walked with us as guide or porter through the forest, our safety, and on occasions our lives, depended upon his wisdom and knowledge of the forest. These happy-go-lucky people, sometimes desperately poor and often sick and afraid of evil spirits, were loyal and faithful workmen. When they became Christians, as many of them did, they expressed their warmth and love and appreciation for what the missionary had to offer them, not just educationally but spiritually.

Five of the happiest years of my missionary service were spent in Liberia and Spanish Guinea under the auspices of the Worldwide Evangelization Crusade. I look back often to those years and thank the Lord for the experiences and the spiritual lessons I learned there, which later I had the privilege of sharing with students during the twenty-five years I taught in three mission Bible Institutes in France, Guatemala and Belgium.

Finally we got our mail from the post office. The customs inspector cleared our baggage and we were ready for the road. Now the hassle began among the porters as to who was going to carry what. A headman from among them was appointed by Mr. Davey and he did not carry anything. His responsibility was to see that every other porter carried what he, the headman, considered to be a legitimate load, about 60 pounds. All the years I spent in Africa, walking behind porters carrying heavy loads of sixty pounds or more, hour after hour, day after day, often not eating until sunset, I never understood how they did it. I remember once trying to carry a load of about thirty pounds on my head for half a mile. I thought my head was going to burst, and I had a stiff neck for several days.

At that time porters were paid fifteen cents a day and given a daily ration of about a pound of rice. It seemed so little to pay them for the hard work they did, but then we missionaries were only receiving forty dollars a month. When we spent three or four weeks on an evangelistic trip it cost us nearly half our allowance to pay and feed our porters. We too had to eat!

When the headman had finished assigning loads

to each porter and all were finally satisfied our party of ten whites and sixty porters started out for Gaypeter station, thirty miles inland. It was quite a sight to see those porters strung out two hundred yards along the path with us following behind. We caused no small stir as we wended our way through Buchanan and into the bush.

Mr. Davey had carefully given instructions to the headman where we would stop for a meal. But when we arrived at the rendezvous, we discovered that several of the porters, including the one carrying the food and utensils, had taken a different path. They had decided to take a shorter route to Gaypeter and we never did catch up with them until that evening.

So there we were without food and utensils. One of the porters offered to go back a couple of miles to buy rice in a larger village we had passed through. The people in the village where we had stopped also offered to sell us some rice, and someone discovered he had several tins of corned beef in his personal baggage!

The headman of the village brought us several huge iron pots and the rice was soon cooked, which when flavored with the corned beef and hot peppers and palm oil, was very edible. We were all very hungry and enjoyed it immensely. For plates we used banana leaves and for forks we used the five that God had put on each hand. Mr. Davey was embarrassed about the whole situation but for us new missionaries it was a lot of fun and somehow seemed appropriate for our first meal in the bush!

Four more hours walking in the afternoon brought us to a German Seventh Day Adventist mission station. The German missionaries had returned to Germany, fearing that Liberia would enter the war on the side of the Allies, which she did later. A small «dash» to the native caretaker procured us comfortable sleeping quarters and for supper we did have the kind of meal the Mission director had planned for us. So with aching muscles after our unaccustomed sixteen-mile walk, and with full tummies, we slept the sleep of the just.

Fourteen more miles walking the next day and we arrived at Gaypeter. Word had been passed along the trail by «bush telephone» (tom-toms) that we were coming. About a mile from the mission station we were met by a large group of excited school children and some of the local people. The children could scarcely contain themselves and sang and danced all the way to the station. What a welcome they gave us! Tired and sunburned we finally came out of the bush into the clearing that was Gaypeter station, and which was to be our home for several weeks until we would be assigned to one of the other stations or to a new one.

Gaypeter station consisted of several acres of cleared forest with one missionary dwelling and a second in the course of construction. Simple buildings had also been erected for the children's school as well as dormitories and a small clinic. Scores of people came every morning for medical help, so from the first day we arrived I was called upon to help in the clinic.

It was the dry season when we arrived and priority was given to making bricks for new buildings. These were made from clay dug from the numerous ant hills in the area. These ant hills were often fifteen to twenty feet high and made excellent material for brickmaking. The schoolboys and girls helped dig the mud and mixed it with water, using their feet, and then carried it to us to be put into wooden molds 12" × 6" × 6". We could make several hundred a day. The same glutinous clay was used for mortar to lay the bricks. When the walls were finished and covered with mud and dried in the sun, the houses were quite sturdy and comfortable to live in. The joists of the ceiling were placed two or three feet beyond the walls so that the thatched roof sat well beyond the walls leaving plenty of space for ventilation. It also left space for snakes which occasionally slithered up the outside wall and on to the inside of the roof or ceiling joists.

On one occasion a snake fell right on top of the mosquito net of one of the lady missionaries while she was sleeping on her camp cot. Her screams brought Mrs. Davey to her room, which was locked, and all Marian could say was, «Carol, there is a big snake coiled on the top of my mosquito net and I don't know what to do.»

«Don't do anything,» Mrs. Davey told her. «I'll get one of the fellows to help you.» She did and Herb climbed up over the wall of the bedroom, thankful there was no ceiling to remove, and dropped down into the bedroom armed with a stout stick to kill the snake. It was still comfortably coiled on the net just a few inches from Marian's face.

«Cover your arm with the blanket and knock it onto the floor so I can kill it,» Herb told her. With one courageous upward push the snake was thrown to the ground and was promptly killed. There is a happy ending to this story. Herb and Marian were married a couple of years later!

It was during my first months at Gaypeter that I led my first African to Christ. He was a twelve-year old boy, son of Bue Sa Dyi, paramount chief of River Cess, an area in which I would later help to open a new WEC station. Alfie wanted desperately to go to school and not remain a bushman all his life. But his father, who was a powerful and wealthy chief, could not read or write and didn't see why his son should be so anxious to have an education. After all, Alfie would be chief some day himself.

«Please send me to the white man's school,» Alfie begged his father almost every day, but Bue Sa Dyi wouldn't listen to him.

Then one day the District Commissioner came to Bue Sa Dyi's town. Alfie immediately went to him and pleaded with him to make his father send him to school. The Commissioner was very much impressed by the boy's earnestness and commanded Bue Sa Dyi to send his son to the mission school in Gaypeter. Alfie, accompanied by two of his father's guards, arrived at Gaypeter two days later «to learn book» at the white man's school.

When I arrived at Gaypeter Alfie had already spent almost a year in school and spoke very good English. One evening as I was sitting on a bench about 100 yards from the main buildings, it had suddenly gotten dark and I realized it was a rather foolish thing to be sitting there alone, not too far from the forest. We had been told that there were many leopards in the forest around Gaypeter, and the thought of meeting one of these big cats made me decide to get back to the house.

Just as I got up from the bench I heard a noise in the bush not too far from where I had been sitting. My hair literally stood up! I was scared and my knees felt weak. Then all of a sudden an African boy jumped out from the bush and yelled, «Oi». It was Alfie. I was both relieved and a little bit angry because he had really scared me. But I was mighty glad it was not a leopard.

When I told him how much he had frightened me, he laughed and said, «Teacher Bob, it is not eating time for Mr. Leopard. He only comes when we are all asleep, and he likes goats and sheep better than people.» I just hoped that Mr. Leopard would always stick to his proper menu!

«What were you doing down here alone?» Alfie asked me.

«Oh, I was waiting for supper and thinking how beautiful God's creation is.» It was a beautiful, starlit, tropical night with a full moon.

Alfie then asked me, «Where is God's town? Where does he live?» When I tried to explain to him, his next question was, «Can people go there in an airplane?»

«No,» I said, «They can't. They have to walk the Jesus way, because Jesus said, 'I am the way, the truth and the life. No man cometh unto the Father, except by me.» (John 14:6)

«How does a person walk the Jesus way?» was his next question.

At that time the New Testament had not yet been translated into the Bassa language, only the Gospel of John. So I explained to him the way of salvation, which he seemed to understand clearly. Then I asked him to accept Jesus into his heart.

«All right, I will,» he said, but I will ask Him in my own language. God does understand Bassa, doesn't He?»

I assured him that God understood Bassa. After he had finished praying (and I didn't understand a word he prayed), I asked him, «What did you ask God to do for you?»

«Oh, I asked Jesus to come into my heart and to clean out all the dirt, and help me walk in the Jesus way.»

«Do you think Jesus has done that?» I questioned him.

«Oh, yes, He wouldn't tell a lie, would He?» he asked me.

«No, no,» I assured him. «Jesus wouldn't tell a lie. Jesus cannot tell a lie!»

I was convinced he had received the Lord. Just a few weeks ago I met a missionary from Liberia, who had seen Alfie recently, and after these many years, he is still walking in the light, on the Jesus way, although physically he is blind.

We worked six days a week, eight to ten hours a day. Praise God there were no trade union restrictions and, like the Israelites when they rebuilt the walls of Jerusalem under Nehemiah's leadership, «Every man and every woman set their hand to the work». Sundays were spent walking in a ten-mile radius from the mission station, preaching the gospel with the aid of an interpreter.

Using interpreters, however, became a crutch and a bad crutch, because most of the missionaries in Liberia did not learn to speak the language and were constantly dependent upon native interpreters. I'm sure it hindered the progress of the work. It certainly hindered the missionaries from getting closer to the people and understanding their culture. I became keenly aware of this after I left Liberia and arrived in Cameroon. I saw that every missionary in the Presbyterian Mission, irrespective of the particular work he was engaged in, doctor, school teacher, dentist, industrial worker, spoke the Bulu language quite effectively. More of this later.

After spending seven months at Gaypeter we new missionaries were assigned to new posts. Janet and two of the girls were assigned to work among the Gio people in the northern part of the State. Three Canadian fellows who arrived soon after us were assigned to work at Gaypeter. Bill and Edith Freeman, Jack Lenny and I were assigned to open a new mission station in the River Cess area about two days' walk from Gaypeter.

Jack and I set out ahead of the Freemans to find a place to live. They followed us a few weeks later. We had no idea of the density of the population in that particular area. In fact, we did not know where the villages lay. On the second day we stopped in a good-sized village called Charlie Cheeseman's town. Many of the villages took their name after the head-man of the village, and often they had strange names. I don't know where old Charlie got his surname because there was no cheese in the country, and he had probably never seen cheese in his life.

Charlie was a friendly fellow although pagan through and through. A number of his people became believers, but not he. He was delighted when we asked him if we could live in his village, and immediately he gave us a fairly decent house to live in. Our presence brought him and his village a lot of prestige—something we did not realize at the time. The people brought us gifts of fruit, rice and chickens, and were eager to hear God's Word. We had services morning and evening in the palaver house in the middle of the village, and one of the first to confess Christ as Saviour was a soldier named Goa.

Goa was a very unusual fellow. He was a big rascal, as many of the native soldiers were. Part of their duty was to collect taxes in the form of rice from the people. Like Zacchaeus, the publican, they often exacted more than they were supposed to, and the people feared and hated them. I don't ever remember meeting any of these soldiers in the bush without his being accompanied by a boy carrying a basket on his head, filled with chickens or a bag of rice, that he had taken from the villagers where he had collected government taxes. I extracted teeth for a number of them, and they always showed their appreciation by giving us several chickens or rice that we knew had been unlawfully taken from some poor bushman. And Goa was no exception.

It caused quite a sensation when Goa accepted Christ as his Saviour. He changed his manner of living and became an enthusiastic disciple of Christ. We taught him to read his Bassa language and he practically memorized the Gospel of John. We had great hopes for him and prayed that he would become an evangelist to his own people.

Satan, however, was also interested in Goa and had great hopes for him. Goa's father was a tribal witch-doctor and also had great hopes for his son. He naturally thought that his son would follow in his footsteps and become a witch-doctor like himself.

These witch-doctors had great authority and the people stood in awe of them. They apparently possessed satanic powers to perform all kinds of unbelievable things. They had power to «witch» people—put them under a spell or a curse—which often caused their deaths, probably because of the fear of the witch-doctor. They were called upon to decide «palavers»—cases where stealing, lying, adultery and so forth were involved—and often the witch-doctor exposed the guilty person, using various diabolical means to do so.

Goa's father was furious when he learned that his son had become a follower of the Lord Jesus Christ instead of Satan. He did everything in his power to entice his son and cause him to fall into sin and deny his faith in Christ. We were not aware of all of this or we would have prayed more earnestly for Goa and warned him against these satanic attacks.

Jack and I went off on a two-weeks' preaching trip and left the Freemans in the village. On our return, as we approached the village we heard the noise of drums and people singing and dancing. When we entered the village just before nightfall, it seemed to us that diabolical forces were at work. The whole village, men, women and children—with a few exceptions—were horribly drunk. You talk about being discouraged; our spirits were low as we watched those who had professed faith in Christ, now drunk and engaged in sensual dancing. After supper we went over to the Freeman's house at the other end of the village and learned that Goa was the principal actor in all that was happening at that moment.

Goa had gone to visit his father, who lived alone in the forest. His father induced him to drink rum and to practice all kinds of witchcraft rituals. It appeared he had become possessed and had returned to Cheeseman's village, and threatened to kill anyone who came near him. Some of his drunken neighbors had succeeded in tying him, and several times they tried to exorcise the evil spirit by pouring hot water over his almost naked body. When we saw him a few hours later we were sure that he was possessed by an evil spirit. What had happened to him, we wondered. Was he like the man whom Jesus described in the Gospels, who was possessed by an unclean spirit and liberated, but the unclean spirit finding seven others more unclean than itself returned to possess the man, whose latter state was worse than before? Is this what had happened to Goa?

The drunken revelry continued all night. The atmosphere seemed charged with evil. We found it impossible to sleep. About midnight we heard piercing screams coming from the direction of Goa's house. I went into Jack's bedroom to see if he were sleeping. He wasn't and had also heard the screams.

«What do you think is happening out there?» I asked him.

«I don't know, Bob, but it sounds like they are killing Goa. We ought to go over and see what's going on,» he replied.

«O.K. Let's go,» I said.

We lit a lamp and went over to the Freeman's house. They also were awake and afraid of what was happening. I told Bill we were going to find out what they were doing to Goa. «Good,» he said, «I would go with you but Edith is scared and I don't like to leave her alone, but if you need me, call me and I'll come immediately.»

We were scared too, but we were not admitting it. Jack and I proceeded to Goa's house. In the darkness we couldn't quite see what was happening. As our eyes got accustomed to the darkness we located Charlie Cheeseman among the crowd, and he was quite drunk.

«What is going on? What are they doing in Goa's house?» I asked Charlie.

«Oh, teacher,» he replied. «Goa is full of the devil and they are trying to get the devil out of him!»

«How?» we asked him.

«Oh, by pouring hot water over him,» Charlie said.

We forced our way inside the house and a horrible sight met our eyes. Goa was spread-eagled on the floor and four men were sitting on top of him, while a fifth was pouring hot water over his body. This was the reason for the screaming we had heard. He was rigid and moaning with pain. We pushed the men off his body but were not sure whether or not he was conscious.

«Goa,» we shouted. «Can you hear us? We have come to help you and pray for you.»

Charlie Cheeseman pushed his way towards us. «How can you help him?» he asked us. «He is full of the devil. Can God send the devil out of him?» he leered at us.

Jack and I felt that Charlie's taunt was a challenge to all that we had taught and preached for nearly nine months in his village.

«Yes,» we answered. «God can help him, and if God wishes, He can chase the demon out of him, and we are going to pray that He will do just that.»

Jack and I started praying for Goa in a loud voice and we both prayed for several minutes. In the meantime the Freemans joined us and they, too, prayed for Goa's deliverance. Suddenly we felt his rigid body go limp and his muscles relax. Slowly he rose to his feet and he was a pitiable sight. Everyone had become very quiet and they were intently looking at him.

«Has God healed him?» Charlie asked us.

«Yes, we believe he has.»

«Then why doesn't he talk? Can't God loosen his tongue?» Goa had tried to talk to us but his words sounded guttural and incoherent.

«Yes, God can loosen his tongue and we are going to pray again for him,» we answered.

We prayed again—all four of us—and before we had finished praying Goa was also praying and praising God for having delivered him from Satan's power. It was a miracle that God performed before our eyes. We took care of his burns, and the next day it was a very subdued Goa who came to us and told us all that had happened to him in his father's house, but he could not remember anything that happened after he got back to Cheeseman's village until the moment we prayed for him. If we hadn't prayed for him, and if God hadn't intervened, he would surely have died.

Goa became a real witness for Christ, but sad to say he did not live long. Several months after his miraculous deliverance he was murdered in the bush. We have reason to believe his death was instigated by his father or some of the tribes people with whom he had formerly practised witchcraft. They may have been afraid that he would reveal some of their secret rituals. I like to believe, at least, that he died because of his faith in Christ. He was the first professing believer in River Cess.

I spent nearly two years working in River Cess. It was very interesting that the Lord led us to settle in Charlie Cheeseman's village. During the first months we lived there, Jack and I made a number of exploratory trips to find out where the people lived. After we had finally located all the villages in the area, we discovered that the Lord had led us to Cheeseman's village because it was located right in the center of the population.

We decided to build our mission station on a hill about a mile from the village. It seemed an ideal spot as there was plenty of timber and numerous ant hills, the two basic materials necessary for building the station. A good-sized stream flowed around the hill guaranteeing a good water supply all year round. We would not need to dig wells. Percy Clubine, our field leader, was due to visit us and we were waiting for his coming before making any final decision. There was one area that we had not fully explored and the people there had sent word asking us to come and build near them. We intended to visit this area along with Percy when he came.

A week later the three of us set off to visit this area. Part of our trek brought us down to the coast and we followed the path along the shore for eight miles, arriving at the mouth of the River Cess as it enters the sea. The canoe crossing was a hundred and fifty yards up the bank from the mouth of the river.

It was extremely hot and the water looked inviting. I had swum across the River Cess many times inland, so I told Clubine and Lenny that I would swim across while they went up to cross in the canoe. I guess the river was 75 yards wide. I plunged in and began swimming to the other side. About half way across I noticed a log floating some 20 yards from me. I didn't pay too much attention to it until I thought I saw it move upstream! Then it moved towards the same bank to which I was heading. My heart almost stopped and one horrible thought penetrated my mind, «Crocodile». My first reaction was to swim like mad, but then a voice seemed to say to me, «Take it easy, don't splash or you will attract the reptile to you.»

I prayed for strength and quietly but fearfully swam slowly towards the shore, keeping my eye all the time upon the «log» until I had scrambled weak and breathless onto the bank. The «log» quietly returned to the middle of the river. All I could do was praise the Lord for overruling my naivete and foolishness in presuming upon His grace.

When Jack and Percy rejoined me, bringing my clothes because I had swum in my underwear, they asked me how I enjoyed my swim.

«I didn't,» I told them, «because I think I saw a crocodile about 20 to 30 yards from me all the time I swam across, but I am not sure—maybe it was just a log.»

«Oh, it was a crocodile, all right. We saw it and were praying for you. You could have been killed,» Percy said.

«I know, and I am going to tell you something, brethren, I will never swim again in an African river, at least not by choice.»

Later we stopped at a German trading post and the proprietor invited us to join him for lunch, which was eaten on a veranda above his store. On the walls of the veranda were a number of large crocodile skins.

«Where did you buy your crocodile skins?» Clubine asked the trader.

«I didn't buy them; I shot them a short while ago down at the mouth of the river,» he said.

Jack then spoke to the trader, and pointing his finger at me said, «This fellow just swam across there an hour ago.»

The trader stopped eating, his fork halfway to his mouth, and with an incredulous look on his face said, «Mister, are you crazy?»

«I think I was until an hour ago, but I have been cured of my craziness,» I told him. He just shook his head and gave me a weak smile. I don't think he believed me, but I knew I was cured!

When we returned to Cheeseman's village, Percy Clubine agreed that we should locate the River Cess station on the hill we had indicated. It was only a mile from our village. We immediately started to work the next day clearing the brushwood and trees to have room to make bricks. We made the trip twice daily, which took a lot of time. So Jack and I decided to build a rough shelter on the hill and live there in order to eliminate the four mile walk every day and save time. In this way we could begin work an hour or two earlier and work as late as we wished. We had difficulty getting help for making the bricks, and it would be a lot cooler to make these in the early hours of the day before the sun became too hot. So we moved our belongings to the hill.

Two young boys, ten and twelve years old, wanted to work for us as personal boys and came up from the village to the hill to live with us. They were practically naked, so my first job was to make pants for them. I didn't quite know how to go about doing this; then I thought, «Why not rip out a pair of my own and get the pattern and simply make them smaller?» It worked and the boys were thrilled with their shorts, which happened to be the first they had ever worn.

We had a lot of fun living on the hill. It was like camping all the time, but much more exciting. At the end of the day's work it was very pleasant—especially on moonlight nights—to relax and listen to the sounds of the jungle. Down at the bottom of the hill where the stream flowed, a large congregation of monkeys would assemble every evening in that spot. Often we could hear their grunts and screams when something annoyed them. We got quite used to their presence and their noises never woke us once we were asleep. And that was our routine, day after day, night after night, for several weeks—until the night the leopards came.

At this point I ought to describe the shelter we lived in. It was not really a shelter in the true sense of the word. It was simply a roof of palm thatch supported by wall poles one foot apart, and a heavy pole in the center of the roof at the front and back. The back and front were completely open. It was twenty feet long and ten feet wide. Sleeping in the shelter was not much different from sleeping in an open field. On moonlight nights we could easily see across the hill through the poles of the shelter.

We slept on canvas camping cots on each side, and our two house boys slept on grass mats between our beds. Life was simple and housekeeping was easy. Native people from nearby villages brought chickens and eggs and fruit for sale, and occasionally a hunter brought deer or wild boar. The River Cess was not far away so we could procure fish easily. We had a good all round diet and lived well off the land, and enjoyed robust health.

It was a moonless night when the leopards decided to pay us a visit. I found myself suddenly awake in the middle of the night, listening intently, and then it came—a sound I had never heard before, but had heard about—the barking of a leopard.

It must have been the barking of the beast that first woke me. Jack also woke up and said, «Hey, what was that?»

«Jack, I don't know what it is, but it sounds like the bark of a leopard, and he is not far away,» I answered.

«Bob, get up and light the lamp,» Jack shouted.

Light the lamp? I had forgotten where we had put it the night before, and I had no idea where the matches were. The two boys were softly crying and saying over and over, «The leopard is going to eat us, the leopard is going to eat us.»

The wicked thought that entered my mind was, «He will come in and take the boys and leave us.»

We started praying and reminding ourselves of God's promise of protection, «The angel of the Lord encampeth round about them that fear him, and he delivereth them.» We prayed for deliverance and God answered our prayers in what can only be regarded as miraculous.

The previous day we had been burning a lot of brushwood on the hill to make room for more building. A strong wind had sprung up and suddenly a pile of logs that had been smouldering burst into flame and illuminated the whole hill. The flames from this bonfire undoubtedly frightened away the leopard because his barking became more and more faint as it moved off into the forest.

When we thought the leopard had really gone, we jumped out of our cots and piled more wood on the fire. For the rest of the night we sat around the fire and drank tea and praised God for sending His angel to deliver us. It was an unforgettable experience.

The next morning, as soon as light broke, our two boys went back to their village and spread the word around about the leopard's visit. A group of men came up from the village along with Bill Freeman, and sure enough they found the marks of the animal's paws—not of one leopard, but of two—all around the shelter. That same day, with the help of these men, we reinforced the «walls» all around the shelter, put a stout door on the front, and borrowed a gun! The leopards never came back. Perhaps they were just as scared of us (or the angel of the Lord), as we were of them. But it was a night to be remembered, and just writing about it thirty-eight years later makes my heart beat a little faster.

We had many answers to prayer that were less spectacular than the one just mentioned. Our tea supply ran out and, although there is coffee grown in Liberia by many of the natives, we never seemed to be able to buy any that was usable. For several weeks we had nothing but boiled water to drink with our meals, and boiled water is not the most palatable drink in the world.

One day I said, «You know, Jack, we pray for all sorts of things we need and yet we have not asked the Lord to send us coffee, why don't we pray for some?» And we did.

Several weeks later a Mandingo tribesman came to the hill for medical help. He was accompanied by his fourteen year old son. The boy was suffering from a toothache and his father had a stiff neck. Could we help them?

I knew I could extract the boy's tooth easily enough, but we had practically no medicine for the man's muscular pain in his neck. I said to Jack, «I wish I could concoct some good old Sloan's Liniment for this fellow's complaint.» Then I thought, «Why not crush some strong red peppers»—we had lots of these growing behind the shelter—«and mix them with palm oil?» This we did and I massaged his neck with the mixture and it seemed to give him a lot of relief. I gave him some of my medicine and told his son to continue to rub his father's neck the way I had done and it would get better. I'm still not sure whether it was the pepper oil or the psychological effect, but he said his neck was healed. They expressed their appreciation and left.

I said to Jack after they had gone, «I wish he had expressed his appreciation in a more practical way like our Bassa people do.» I felt rebuked the next day when our Mandingo friend turned up again with his boy to greet us. He gave us several chickens and took a bag off his boy's shoulder and handed it to me. It contained about twenty pounds of coffee! That night we had coffee with our meal instead of boiled water.

I had another unforgettable experience while in River Cess. In the rainy season Jack and I spent a lot of time trekking through the villages, preaching the gospel, as we could not do any building on the hill. On one of these trips we stopped in a village for a meeting and called the people to the palaver house. This was usually a large open space covered by a roof that sat on four stout poles. The villagers often cooked in these houses and met to talk and dance and sing. We often slept in these shelters on treks, and we almost always had our meetings in the palaver house. I have already mentioned that we only had the Gospel of John translated into the Bassa language. So most of our preaching and teaching was based on this Gospel. We encouraged the people— especially the young people—, to come to the mission station and learn how to read it for themselves. They were often amazed to realize that the stories we told them were actually written in their Bassa language.

On this particular occasion I was using John 3:14 as a text, explaining the story of the disobedience of the Israelites in the wilderness and how God punished them, but at the same time provided a remedy for them to be healed through looking at the brass serpent, relating it to the death of Christ on the cross. It usually took a long time to explain, using an interpreter, and the people always patiently waited until we had finished speaking before they asked questions. It was considered very impolite to ask a question while the other person was still speaking. It was only done when the question was considered to be very important. So we were hardly ever interrupted while we spoke. When they did wish to interrupt they stood to their feet and waited to be asked what they wished to say. There were about twenty-five people listening quietly as I told them the Bible story. Slowly an old man rose to his feet and lifted his hand as a sign he wished to speak.

«What do you wish to say, old man?» I asked him.

«Just one question, white man,» he said. «Is that small book you hold in your hand really God's Word written in my language?» I assured him it was.

«Read it to me,» he said. And I read him John 3: 14-16. It was the first time he had ever heard those words, and when I came to the 16th verse I read it very slowly,

> For God so loved the world that he gave his only begotten son, that whosoever believeth in him should not perish, but have everlasting life.

I shall never forget his reaction. Covering his mouth with his hand he let out a long *aiiiiii* sound, something the Bassas did when they were surprised or astonished.

«Old man, do those words surprise you?» I asked him.

«They are sweet,» he replied. «They are sweet! Read them to me again.» And I read them a second time, and a third time.

«Old man, do you believe these words? Do you believe in Jesus?» I then asked him.

«Oh, I believe, I believe, I believe,» he said. Then he turned to the others in the palaver house and said to them, «For a long, long time I have wanted to hear words like these; now I have heard them with my own ears and I believe them.»

I am convinced that he really believed, even though it was the first time, apparently, that he had heard the gospel story. His experience was like the one mentioned in Acts 16:14, «And a certain woman named Lydia, a seller of purple..., which worshiped God heard us and the Lord opened her heart so that she attended unto the things that were spoken of Paul.» I believe that just in the same way that Lydia heard and the Lord opened her heart so that she believed, this old Liberian native also heard the same gospel and the Lord opened his heart so that he believed the things that were spoken to him. The gospel has not changed, neither has God's power changed.

It was almost a year since we had arrived in Liberia and once again Jack and I were out on a preaching trip. On our way back to the hill a runner from Gaypeter station met us and handed me a closed tin in which was a cable from Mr. Grubb in London, asking me to leave Liberia as soon as possible and join my sister Emma in Spanish Guinea. A boat ticket and money would be waiting for me at the British Consulate in Monrovia. A letter of explanation would follow.

It took a week for us to get back to the hill, pack our bags and proceed to Gaypeter. At Gaypeter there was a letter telling me that Emma was alone as Mr. and Mrs. Throne had to return to England and the mission did not want my sister to be alone in Spanish Guinea. The Thornes had spent ten years without a furlough and Emma had already spent seven years and was due to return to England. The WEC wanted to be sure that the mission station in Spanish Guinea would be occupied and the churches cared for. So I was asked to make every effort to reach Spanish Guinea before Emma would be obliged to leave.

I believe if I had known what was going to happen in the attempt to reach Spanish Guinea, I would have been tempted to stay on in Liberia. But if I had stayed, then my missionary career would have been very different. It was with high hopes and excitement that I said farewell to my colleagues at Gaypeter and started out to walk the 100 miles to Monrovia. On the way to the capital, the boy who was carrying my box of books ran off into the forest with them, and I never saw him again. So for the next four years the only book I had in Africa was my Scofield Bible. I had mixed feelings about losing all my books; I would have rather lost any of my other possessions, but the loss was a blessing in disguise because I read my Bible more.

The first night I stopped in a village and a young man came to me and asked me to cut off his toe! I looked down at his feet and sure enough one of his small toes was hanging to his foot by a thread. It was so swollen it looked more like a red cherry than a toe. I decided it would be very simple to put a ligament around it and snip it off. So I sterilized a scalpel and and got some bandages ready. When I was about to perform this little operation, he stopped me and asked me how much I was going to pay him for cutting off his toe. I thought I had misunderstood him and he wanted to know how much he had to pay me with food or otherwise. So I told him, «Nothing, you don't have to pay me anything.»

«Oh,» he said. «Mr. Missionary, you don't understand me. I want to know how much you are going to pay me.» And he pointed to his chest.

«Nothing,» I told him. «I will pay you nothing. I don't care if I cut off your toe or not.»

«All right,» he said. «I will keep my toe.» And he got up and walked away. I have often wondered what happened to his toe, and if someone ever paid him for the privilege of cutting it off.

A couple of days later I arrived in Monrovia and procured my ticket and money from the British Consul. He advised me to get a visa before leaving for Spanish Guinea. He told me there was a Spanish Consul in Monrovia, which greatly surprised me.

I went to the Spanish Consulate, which was an old, dilapidated house, and spoke to an elderly man, who assured me he was the consul all right. I must confess I had misgivings and wondered if he were bluffing me. But he presented some legal stamps and stamped my passport and charged me fifteen dollars.

Weeks later I was to learn to my sorrow that he had been the Spanish Consul under the Spanish Republican regime but since the overthrow of the Republic by General Franco, his stamp and signature on my passport were worthless. However, I was blissfully ignorant of all this at that time, so, without a care in the world, I boarded an American ship going to Lagos, Nigeria, from where I would try to go overland to Cameroon and then south to Spanish Guinea, situated on the Equator.

CHAPTER 5

Attempts To Reach Spanish Guinea

Soon after I boarded the ship I met the captain, who told me that there was another passenger on board besides myself. «A dumb foreigner», he said, «and none of us can understand him.» I learned there was just one cabin for passengers on this ship, so I went down to meet my cabin-mate, the dumb foreigner!

I discovered that my cabin-mate was a Spaniard who spoke no English, but was quite fluent in French. When I spoke to him in French his eyes lit up and a torrent of words poured forth. Poor fellow, for days he had not been able to communicate with anyone and felt very frustrated. For me it looked like he was a direct answer to my unspoken prayer to be able to meet someone who could teach me the rudiments of the Spanish language. It seemed like the Lord had guided me so wonderfully and yet, unknown to me, there were strange adventures lying ahead of me on this trip.

It took the ship almost a month to reach Lagos. The distance was not the reason for the long trip, but the many delays en route. It seemed wherever there was a trading post along the coast, the ship stopped to unload cargo. Then we were also delayed because of wartime restrictions. German subs were sinking ships all along the African coast. I have already mentioned the sinking of the *M.V. SANGARA* off the coast of Ghana. Even though our ship was American, with a huge flag of the stars and stripes painted on the sides of the vessel, as well as being brightly illuminated at night, danger from submarines was always there. Submarine commanders often didn't take time to distinguish between allied ships and others.

But I enjoyed every moment of it and my cabin companion was quite congenial and ready to help me with my Spanish study. This happy state of affairs lasted for two weeks until we reached Accra, in Ghana. It was here that I was to experience the first of several frustrating and inexplicable circumstances, some of which I have only understood in the light of God's sovereignty.

As soon as the ship anchored in Accra it was boarded by several English and Free French military officers, who informed the captain that they had come aboard to question his passengers. We were called to the dining room to meet them and the officer in charge said to me, «We will talk to your Spanish friend first and you later; please wait outside.»

An hour later I saw two policemen leading my

Spanish cabin-mate away. One of the policemen was carrying his suitcase. I began to experience a strange feeling of fear and anxiety. What was wrong? I was soon to find out.

An officer came out of the dining room and beckoned me to enter. Four or five of the officers were seated around the table like they were holding court and they began to fire questions at me. What had I been doing in Liberia? Why was I traveling with this Spaniard? Why was I traveling with a false Spanish visa issued by an unauthorized person? This was the first time my fears were confirmed about the seedy-looking Spanish consul in Liberia. I was amazed the British Consul had insisted I get that visa, which apparently was worthless even though it cost me fifteen dollars. It was going to cost me more before long. When I tried to explain to them what had happened, I was told, «Perhaps you had better keep your explanation for another time. In the meantime you are not permitted to leave this ship.» And they handed me back my passport.

To say I was troubled was putting it mildly. I went down to my cabin feeling very low and apprehensive, wondering what they meant by «another time». I couldn't quite figure it out, except that it had something to do with my Spanish cabin-mate. It had!

After dinner that evening the captain, who seemed to have taken a liking to me, said, «Bob, it looks like you might be in a spot of trouble. Let me tell you something; when you talk with these johnnies in Lagos, that Spanish fellow they took away; they think he is a spy, and they are not sure how well you know him or how much you are implicated with him. I told them you had never met him until you got on board my ship in Monrovia, but I am warning you, they may give you a hard time in Lagos.»

We arrived two weeks later in Lagos and sure

enough the same scenario took place. I was immediately summoned by a military officer who told me to follow him. He was accompanied by a burly Nigerian police sergeant. I descended the gangway with them, got into their car and was driven to what I suppose was either a police barracks or military camp. I was led into an office there and questioned for nearly two hours by two men in civilian clothes. It was rather unreal in some ways and I kept asking myself, «Do they really suspect me of being a spy?» I had heard of this sort of thing but had never personally experienced it.

«Where were you born?»

«In Belfast, Northern Ireland.»

«How long did you live there?»

«Twenty years.»

«Name the main streets of your city.»

I did.

«How long did you live in London?»

«Four years.»

«Why did you go to France?»

«To study.»

«How many times did you visit Spain?»

«I was never there.»

«Why did you study French?»

«To go to the Ivory Coast as a missionary.»

«Why didn't you go there?»

«The war prevented me.»

«How long have you lived in Liberia?»

«One year.»

«Name the Germans whom you know there.»

«I don't know any of them personally,
    so I don't know their names.»

«Why are you going to Spanish Guinea?»

88

The questioning lasted nearly two hours. Finally I said to them, «Why are you interrogating me in this manner?»

«Because we do not believe you,» they answered.

I didn't know whether to laugh or be afraid. They had my passport and I was certainly at their mercy. They had the power to retain me and do whatever they thought they should.

«Look,» I said, «why do you think I speak English with an Irish accent?»

«Well,» they replied, «that is no problem for a German spy.» I could not help but laugh at that statement.

«Listen,» I told them, «I was born in Belfast, Northern Ireland. I attended Jennymount School and the Belfast Technical College; I spent two years in the Bible College of Wales, Swansea and one year in the Missionary School of Medicine in Great Ormond Street, London, and eight months in France.» I gave the addresses where I had lived. «I am a bona fide member of the Worldwide Evangelization Crusade, whose headquarters are in London and whose General Secretary is Mr. Norman Grubb. My sister lives in Acurenan, Spanish Guinea and I am on my way to join her. You can have any of these statements verified by your intelligence service in London. Now can I go?»

«Yes,» they told me. «You can go back to the ship and retrieve your luggage and then go and stay at the Southern Baptist Mission Academy in Lagos until your ship goes back to Monrovia. When it leaves next Saturday, you will leave with it, and our advice to you is, don't leave Liberia again until the war is over.»

I spent the next week in Lagos accompanied everywhere by a fine Nigerian policeman. As soon as I walked out of the Academy, he was there to greet me with a big smile. He was a Christian and actually we had a great time together. On Saturday when I boarded the ship he was there to wave goodbye to me. I felt I had left at least one friend behind me in Lagos.

Two weeks later the ship anchored off the Liberian coast at the mouth of the St. John River, where Mr. Davey met me. A few days later I returned to Gaypeter and went back again to River Cess to rejoin Jack and the Freemans after my abortive attempt to reach Spanish Guinea. This time I really felt ready and willing to spend the rest of my missionary life in the Republic of Liberia. Emma, I learned later, had returned to Ireland and I must confess I put the idea of ever going to Spanish Guinea out of my mind completely. I enthusiastically flung myself into the work of evangelizing the Bassa people in River Cess.

We completed the first missionary building on the hill soon after I arrived. Jack and I resumed our gospel trips into the surrounding villages. I opened a small clinic and attended the sick and extracted teeth and this was our routine for several months.

One morning a patient told me he had no money or anything to pay for his medicine, but he did have a «Bible book» he would like to give me. Having lost all my books I was grateful to have anything to read. The Bible book turned out to be an Episcopal Book of Common Prayer. I was delighted to have it, as I had been brought up in the Episcopal Church of Ireland and knew many of the collects and prayers by heart; they are not only beautiful but Biblical. I enjoyed reading it on occasions, although I was Baptist by conviction.

Bill Freeman often teased me about reading my prayers! When I asked him if he would like to borrow it, he grinned and said, «Bob, when I need that prayer book, I'll have to be too weak to pray and you will have to come and read it to me.»

He said this as a joke, of course, but not too long afterwards Bill had a violent attack of malaria. He ran a very high fever and one evening Edith came over to our house and said, «Bob, come over and see if you can do something for Bill, his temperature is very high and I think he is delirious.»

Jack and I went over to see him and I took his temperature and it was nearly 105°. His face was crimson and his body was burning. I did everything I knew how, to bring down his temperature, but it continued to stay up. I thought his wife was exaggerating when she said he was delirious, but a moment later I realized she might have been right, because Bill looked at me rather sternly and said, «Bob Munn, go get your prayer book and read me a prayer.»

At first I thought he was joking and didn't make any move to go for the prayer book. There he spoke to me again and this time quite severely, «Don't you understand what I have just asked you to do? Why don't you get that prayer book and read a prayer to me?» To humor him I went back to the house and got the prayer book. When I returned to his house I asked him what prayer he wished for me to read.

«Oh, any you wish,» he said.

I casually opened the prayer book and read the first prayer my eyes fell on: «Lighten our darkness we beseech Thee O Lord, and by Thy great mercy defend us from all the perils and dangers of this night for the sake of Thine only Son, Jesus Christ our Lord. Amen.»

As I read it a second time, I could not help thinking how apropos this prayer was for us at that particular moment. There we were in the African bush with a very sick missionary, far from professional medical help and only the Lord to call upon for help. I said to the others, «Why don't we really pray this prayer instead of reading it?» In unison we prayed, «Defend us from all the perils and dangers of this night.»

When we finished praying that prayer, Bill was perspiring profusely. He was soaked and looked like he had fallen into the River Cess! His temperature fell and in a few days he was his old self again and back on the building site.

About a year after I returned to Liberia I had to go to Gaypeter on a business trip. During the several days I was there I went out on a short evangelistic trip with one of the Canadian fellows. It was what the natives called «hungry time», i.e., several weeks before the rice harvest was gathered. It was hard to buy rice and our diet consisted mostly of manioc, sweet potatoes and bananas; we had a hard time, sometimes, even to buy these. We also had little response in our meetings; the people seemed lethargic and uninterested. Sometimes we only had half a dozen come to the meetings and often we simply went out to their farms and spoke to individuals or families.

One evening I said to my Canadian colleague, «Say, do you think we'll ever evangelize these people before the Lord returns?»

«Bob,» he answered, «I don't believe we will because I don't think we are using the right methods. I believe we should be spending more time teaching our converts the Word of God, concentrating upon them, and training them how to evangelize their own people. This is a Biblical principle and the apostle Paul used it effectively. Sure, we have to evangelize them, but let us also *make disciples* of them. This is also part of the Great Commission.»

«Look,» he continued, «how many young men Paul

gathered around him and taught them the principles of sharing the Word of God with others. Look what is written of him in Acts 19:9-10, 'But when divers were hardened, and believed not, and spake evil of that way before the multitude, he departed from them and separated the disciples, disputing daily in the school of one called Tyrannus. And this continued for the space of two years; so that all they that dwelt in Asia heard the word of the Lord Jesus, both Jews and Greeks.' And consider what he wrote to the Philippians, 'Those things which ye have both learned and heard and seen in me, do...' Even when he was about to die, he was still thinking of this principle of training others, and thus he wrote to Timothy in II Timothy 2:2, 'And the things that thou hast heard of me among many witnesses, the same commit thou to faithful men, who shall be able to teach others, also.'»

«Bob,» he went on, «you and I should be asking God to give us Timothys to teach. Look at it this way. Here we are, white men, seeking to evangelize the Africans, and by God's grace we are trying to do this. But this is not our country and no matter how much we endeavor to identify ourselves with the nationals, we shall always be foreigners. This is *their* country, *their* culture, *their* language, *their* people. Let us train Africans to evangelize Africans!»

During the months that followed, this conversation would come to my mind over and over again. Maybe this is why God had brought me back again to Liberia to be faced with this challenge. Maybe the Lord would use me to train Africans to reach their own people for Christ. I felt inadequately prepared to do this, simply from a theological point of view. I hadn't had the proper training for this task. Would I be willing to go back to a Bible school and seminary in the United States, where I felt I would get a more practical Bible education than I had had in Britain? But whom do I know in the States? No one. And what school? The only one I had ever heard of at that time was Moody Bible Institute in Chicago. I knew there must be scores of others, but I was not acquainted with any of them. What will my friends say if I tell them—at the end of five years of missionary work in Africa—that I am not prepared for the work I wished to do? Today, it is almost the norm for many missionaries to do refresher courses, but it wasn't the norm then; it was the exception.

But my Canadian colleague had planted a thought in my heart that I could not easily forget. In the ensuing years it became an obsession with me that I must go back and prepare myself for this kind of teaching ministry. When I look back now I know it was the Lord who gave me this desire and burden.

When we got back to Gaypeter station from this short gospel trip, the station leader told me another cable had come for me from London. Before I read it, I knew I was going to be told to make another attempt to go to Spanish Guinea. I was right. That is exactly what the cable said. It was from Mr. Grubb and it read, «Proceed again to Spanish Guinea via Freetown and Douala. Grubb.»

My first reaction was, «They must be out of their mind, after what had happened the first time. They have no idea how difficult it is to travel in wartime and I will end up in jail. Suppose the Lagos police have informed the Freetown immigration about me and my escapade in Lagos.» I could not sleep all night, and found myself praying over and over that the Lord would show me His will.

Then I began to reason, «Well, if the Crusade leaders feel it is the Lord's will for me to go to Spanish Guinea, they must have prayed much about it and discussed it and feel it is feasible. Why should

I doubt it? If the situation calls for some bold action on my part, why not make another attempt to go to Spanish Guinea?»

The next day I talked it over with the senior missionaries and they all agreed I should try to go. Slowly the conviction came to me that this was God's will and He would enable me to overcome whatever difficulties might be ahead. I knew there would be plenty, but I would succeed and arrive safely in Spanish Guinea.

As I walked the second time to Monrovia I must confess from time to time I felt a little apprehensive about the trip. Just to get north to Freetown from Monrovia was no easy task. I knew I would have an extremely hard time finding porters to walk that far, and ships stopping at Monrovia en route to Freetown were few and far between. I had no idea how long I might have to stay in Monrovia.

«And when he putteth forth his own sheep, he goeth before them...» (John 10:4) How true this text was for me during the next weeks! The first indication that he had gone before was a few days after arriving in Monrovia; the captain of a Liberty ship that had called to pick up rubber in the Firestone plantation agreed to take me to Freetown—free— even though there was no passenger accomodation. I slept in the living room of the chief engineer's two-room suite, and this good man loaded me with all kinds of material goods that I could not find in Africa. I shall always remember his kindness to me.

Freetown was filled with thousands of allied seamen and soldiers. I also discovered that there were scores of missionaries waiting for transport to various parts of Africa. Among these I met a Belfast couple whom I knew well. What a joy to meet them and hear firsthand news of my family! I had not received any mail for nearly four months, and had

95

vaguely heard that Belfast had been bombed on two occasions. So my first question was, «How is my family; are they well?»

They looked at one another and then asked me, «Haven't you had any news from your family or any others in Belfast?»

When I answered in the negative, they told me that our two shops and the dwelling houses above them had been completely demolished, but my family had been spared. I have recounted the story, briefly, in Chapter 1. «The angel of the Lord encampeth round them that fear him, and he delivereth them.» How often these words of the Psalmist would come to mind during those war years.

Well, it was almost as difficult to get away from Freetown as it had been from London two and a half years previously. I spent six weeks there and every morning, without fail, made the round of the shipping companies, hoping to get a positive answer that I might be able to get a boat going directly to Douala. There were very few making the direct journey to this port in Cameroon, and I certainly did not wish to stop again in Accra and Lagos.

In Freetown I got to know an English missionary working with The Christian Mission to Seamen. When he learned that I had time on my hands and didn't know when I would leave Freetown, he asked me to help him in his mission. There were plenty of opportunities for witness among the hundreds of servicemen that came to the canteen daily for meals. I served tea and meals, and also preached in the evangelistic services. It filled up the days for me. My friend appreciated my help and promised to do all he could to help me get a passage to Douala. In fact, if it had not been for his intervention, I might have spent the rest of the war years in Freetown! Somehow he had heard of a small ship that was going to Douala, and one evening he took me out on his launch to talk, personally, with the captain. I had discovered that if captains were disposed to take passengers on their ships, they could do so, irrespective of what the shipping companies did, and, of course, it was wartime and they were more sympathetic in helping people move around when the opportunity was available. So I was able to ask the captain if he were going to Douala, and could he take me as a passenger?

«Sure, I am going to Douala, but I have no passenger accomodation on my ship,» he told me.

«Sir,» I told him, «I am willing to join your crew and work my way there.

He looked at me for a long minute and then said, «You know something young man, it is against the Seamens Union rules to hire a non-union member; and besides, you are not even supposed to know that I am leaving Freetown. However, if you wish to share the crew's quarters and don't mind roughing it, you can bring your luggage on tonight, but if you are not on board before midnight, the deal is off.»

«Don't worry, I'll be back in a couple of hours,» I told him.

We got back to shore and I quickly packed my bags and within an hour my English missionary friend was taking me back to the ship well before midnight. What a relief to get on board after six weeks of waiting! It was a small ship, not much bigger than the average tugboat, but it was going directly to Douala and that was all that mattered to me.

Ten days later we arrived in Cameroon, which at that time was a French colony. «As for God his way is perfect.» I was to experience the truth of these words many times in the coming years as I endeavored to obey the Lord and go wherever He wanted me to go.

In Douala I was welcomed by Mr. and Mrs. Ted Cozzens of the American Presbyterian Mission in Cameroon. They had been expecting me to arrive for a long time and, therefore, were not surprised when I landed on their doorstep with a request for help. And what a help they were! They helped me through customs, and they had prepared an old 1931 Chevrolet that Mr. Thorne had left for me to drive to Spanish Guinea. They got me «laissez-passer» from the officials in order for me to drive through Cameroon. They had even bought enough gasoline for the long trip there. The Cozzens knew the Thornes and my sister Emma and, of course, were colleagues of the McNeills in Spanish Guinea, members of their own Presbyterian Mission. They were kindness personified.

One day at lunch Mrs. Cozzens said, «You know, we heard all about your abortive attempt to come here a year ago, and now you have made it. You will love the McNeills and the national Christians, but there is one thing we want to ask you not to do,» and she said this with a big grin. «Please don't take our Elizabeth away from us.»

«Well, who is your Elizabeth?» I asked her. I tried to ask the question as casually as I could as I did not wish to sound too eager or enthusiastic. «Is she good-looking? Does she work in Spanish Guinea with the McNeills?»

«Yes, we think she is good-looking,» Mrs. Cozzens replied. «She is our missionary childrens' school teacher in Elat, but is presently studying Bulu with Lois McNeill in Spanish Guinea. You will meet her down there.»

«Well,» I thought to myself, «this sounds interesting. She is good-looking, doesn't work in Spanish

Guinea or in WEC, but who knows, the Lord might give her a call.» I was definitely interested in Elizabeth!

I left Douala in the old Chevvy and had travelled about 100 miles when the motor conked out and I had no idea how to get it started. I rolled to the bottom of a hill. I had no idea where I was except somewhere between Douala and Elat. No cars had passed me either way. It was five in the afternoon and I knew it would be dark in an hour or two, and it would be dangerous to spend the night in the car. I was reluctant to leave all my stuff and start out to look for a village. So I sat there and prayed for help, wondering how and where the help would come from. I knew I could sit there for several days without a car or anyone passing.

Thirty minutes later I was still praying when a native man emerged from the bush carrying a spear, with a small, dead animal around his neck, followed by two small hunting dogs. As he approached me I wished with all my heart I could communicate with him. Imagine my surprise and joy when he said to me in perfect French, «*Bonjour, monsieur, qu'est-ce qu'il y a. Votre voiture est tombée en panne, n'est-ce pas*? (Good day, Sir, what has happened? Has your car broken down?)»

«Where did you learn to speak French so well?» I asked him.

«In Douala; I worked there for five years.»

«What kind of work did you do?» I enquired.

«I'm a mechanic,» and he grinned at me. «Do you want me to help you get your car started?»

Get my car started? I could have fallen on his neck and kissed him, I was so overjoyed. In a few minutes he had located the difficulty and the car started. His village was a couple of miles further on in the direction I was going, and he asked me for a ride and invited me to stay in his village that night. What an answer to prayer!

The headman of the village welcomed me warmly and gave me a house to sleep in. He brought me food and agreed for me to have a meeting in the palaver house. My mechanic friend was my interpreter. That night I went to bed praising God for what He had done. That native hunter could have emerged anywhere from the bush onto the highway, but the Lord caused him to step out at the spot where I was «en panne»—broken down. It is true he may have heard the sound of the motor in the forest, but it was still a miracle that possibly the only native man within a hundred miles was out hunting at that particular time, and was, to boot, a mechanic! It assured me more than ever that He would take me safely to Spanish Guinea. There is nothing too hard for the Lord. With God all things are possible. All things are possible to him that believeth. There is no greater thrill than to walk in His will, which is always good and perfect and acceptable.

The next day I reached Elat, where the Presbyterian Mission has its largest station. When I rolled into the mission property I thought I was entering a small town. There were several large, well-built missionary houses near the entrance, where was also located the Frank James Industrial School, which employed nearly a thousand men and was managed by Dr. Fred Hope. All the workmen had to be professing Christians, and the majority were true believers. The school taught several trades: ivory and ebony carving, carpentry, tailoring, furniture making and so forth. The church close by, where services for the workmen were held, was the equivalent of any large church in the States. Each worker was required to attend, and Dr. Hope and Mr. Cozzens did the preaching and teaching.

Several hundred yards from the industrial school was located a small cemetery where a number of the early missionaries and some children are buried, including the father of Bob Evans, founder of the Greater Europe Mission. Several hundred yards beyond the cemetery stands what, for many years, was the largest Presbyterian church in the world. This beautiful brick building holds 3,200 people and is packed every Sunday morning. At one time the Elat church boasted 12,000 members. The congregation was obliged to split up into eight large churches in the surrounding area, including the Elat church. In the early years it was necessary to hold three services on Sunday and different colored cards were given for different services.

Beyond the church stood the missionary children's school and dormitory, and close by the school was located the printing press. Half a mile beyond the children's school was the hospital, where several hundred patients were cared for by three missionary doctors and a dentist. The hospital had a full-time evangelist to care for the spiritual needs of the patients. And still further on in the bush was located the leprosarium with several hundred patients in all stages of the disease. I shall never forget the experience of speaking to these lepers on whose disfigured faces shone the beauty of the Lord. What a ministry Doctors Wolfe, Weber and Thorne had among these thousands of Africans who passed through the hospital and leprosarium!

I remember years later, speaking at the first Toccoa Falls missionary conference, Dr. Weber was one of the speakers, and in a discussion about the contribution of medical missions to the evangelization of a country, he said that an average of one person every day accepted Christ in the hospital. «This,» he said, «was our prayer before we ever built the hospital.»

Hundreds came to know Christ through the dedicated service of love shown by these medical men of God.

Shortly after I arrived at the Elat station I was told by the station hostess that I would be staying with Dr. Fred Hope, Elizabeth's father. «Hey,» I thought, «This is great; maybe I'll have a chance to see her photo.» When I entered the house, Dr. Hope was at the industrial school, and I had all the time in the world to inspect the photos of his daughters, and there were scores of them all over the house! There were five girls in the family, and there were pictures of them as babies, grade school scholars, high school and college pictures and, except for the difference in their ages, they all looked alike. I still didn't know which one was Elizabeth.

That evening at supper Dr. Hope said to me, «So you are going down to Spanish Guinea? You will meet my daughter Elizabeth, who is studying Bulu down there.»

«Yes, I guess I will,» I said. The Cozzens told me she was down there staying with the McNeills.

«That's right,» Dr. Hope said. «This is Elizabeth;» he said, pointing to a family picture, «and this is Arta Grace, my oldest daughter, and this is Esther and Roberta and Winifred. I had hoped to have a boy after four girls; when Winifred appeared her mother and I decided to have my name somehow included in hers, so we called her Winifred.»

Well, that night my thoughts were full of Elizabeth. «Now I know at least what she looks like, and she is good-looking. I hope she is as sweet as everybody says and, who knows, maybe I can persuade her to leave the Presbyterian Mission and join the WEC!» This was not to be, but it was with a light heart that I got into my old Chevvy and started out on the last stage of my journey to Bolondo, Spanish Guinea.

Bolondo is situated twenty miles south of Bata on the coast, and that is where the McNeills lived. They had sent me word to say I could live with them as long as I needed in order to learn Spanish and get acquainted with the country. Wonderful, hospitable people, whom I came to love deeply.

I arrived in Bolondo in the company of two other Presbyterian missionaries who were going to spend a week with the McNeills and take Elizabeth back to Cameroon with them. Mac shook hands with me and introduced me to his wife, Lois, and to Don Ramon Ruiz, a Spanish Presbyterian missionary from Madrid, and then to Elizabeth. I know it sounds trite to say so, but I did fall in love with her at first sight. I did not realize at that moment, however, that it would be five long years before we would become man and wife. But I was finally in Spanish Guinea, and somehow I didn't feel quite so lonely as I had felt at times during the ten weeks it took me to reach there. I was in love!

CHAPTER 6

Adventures In
Spanish Guinea

Spanish Guinea, today referred to as Equatorial Guinea and since independence in 1968 called Rio Muni, was one of Spain's former colonies in Africa. Along with the island of Fernando Po in the Gulf of Guinea, where Santa Isabel, the capital of Rio Muni is located, Equatorial Guinea has a land area of some 30,000 square kilometers. This small enclave on the African mainland is situated between Cameroon and the Congo (not Zaire). It has a population of 300,000 of whom the Fang-Okak tribes are politically dominant and number about 215,000.

It was among the Fang-Okak people the Presbyterian and WEC missionaries worked. When the first WEC missionaries entered Rio Muni they were welcomed by Presbyterian missionaries, Joe and Lois McNeill. Mac, as he was called by his associates, was an indefatigable worker, who with his wife spent more than forty years serving the Lord in this little corner of the African continent.

When I arrived «out of the blue» the McNeills welcomed me with open arms. I can never forget the kindness and hospitality which they showered upon me. They were greatly burdened for the believers in the southern part of the colony where the WEC had established a number of churches. Since the departure of Mr. and Mrs. Thorne and my sister Emma, the churches in the south were without any missionary help whatsoever. They sometimes felt isolated from the evangelical communities in the north of the land, and they were despised by the pagan as well as by the Catholic population. The Catholic Church claimed 85 % of the Fang-Okak people as members of their church, and the Catholic priests, both Spaniards and nationals, had endeavored to baptize as many as possible. The small evangelical communities in the south were in the minority, and in some ways suffered from an ecclesiastical, spiritual complex.

Besides his many responsibilities in his own missionary work, Mac occasionally visited the WEC church in Acurenan and spent a weekend with them in order to hold communion with the believers and to encourage them to pray that God would send them a missionary teacher. Most of these believers had been recently won to Christ. They had come out of total paganism, some of which will be explained later. They had very little Bible instruction and the six evangelists who had been ordained as such, even though they were zealous in preaching the gospel and had tried to pastor the churches, were inadequately prepared for that task.

However, they did have one tremendous advantage in that many of them could read and write Spanish and Bulu. Bulu is a Cameroonian language spoken by thousands of people and closely related to the Fang-Okak languages. The Presbyterian missionaries had translated the Bible into Bulu. They had also prepared a Bulu grammar and dictionary, besides the *Pilgrim's Progress,* a good-sized hymnbook with many of the well-known English melodies, and a number of studies and commentaries on various books of the Bible.

Not only was all of this translated literature a wonderful privilege and advantage for the native believers, but for me as well. Here I had at my disposal all I needed to learn the Okak language, which one could do fairly easily by studying Bulu. I very quickly understood much of what the people were saying, and at the end of a year had mastered enough of the language to give a simple Bible message in church each morning. In fact, it was like learning two languages at the same time, with the one helping the other. It was a very unusual as well as an intriguing language situation for me. It meant that later, when I had occasions to visit Cameroon, I could converse and preach in Bulu as well as Okak.

Of course, all this was unknown to me those first three months I spent in Bolondo. The McNeills insisted I stay that long in order to understand Spanish better. I had picked up quite a few phrases from my Spanish cabin-mate during the three weeks we were together on that first ill-fated attempt to reach Rio Muni. Don Ramon Ruiz and Lois McNeill conducted a small school for believers and their children in Bolondo. Lois taught in Bulu and Don Ramon in Spanish. Here again was another ideal language situation for me, because I was exposed to two languages at the same time. The McNeills spoke Spanish in the home most of the time because of Don Ramon's presence. He spoke very little English at that time.

At the end of three months of intensive study I was able to engage in a simple conversation and had a sufficient knowledge to get around in the language. It gave me enough confidence to go into the interior to Acurenan and get involved in the work there.

How can I describe the welcome that was given to me by the believers in Acurenan when I first arrived? I could hardly believe that some of them had walked nearly 100 miles to see «Don Roberto». I was thankful that I could communicate a little bit with them in Spanish.

I spent hours the following week trying to translate a simple message from English Spanish, trying to memorize it, hoping that it would last half an hour. It lasted just over five minutes! But it was my first attempt to preach in Spanish.

Four weeks later I went on a six weeks' preaching trip with three of the evangelists and we visited the whole territory where the WEC had churches in southern Rio Muni. By the time I got back to Acurenan, after having spoken twice, and sometimes three times a day, giving more or less the same message, I felt more fluent in the language and more confident. I had now been in the interior two and a half months. Six months had passed since I had arrived in Spanish Guinea.

I was so busy trying to learn the language and getting acclimated to the situation in which I found myself and getting to know the local populace—Christians and otherwise—that I hardly had time to think about Elizabeth or my family in Ireland. But on the way back from the gospel trek, I kept hoping and praying for mail. Six months had passed since I had had any letters from anyone anywhere. Sure enough, there was a whole sack of mail waiting for me. I quickly searched through the bag for letters from home and there were nearly a dozen from Mother and others in the family. But the news was also six months old.

My mother's letters were the first I read, and I wished I had kept them to the last. In the very first letter I opened, she wrote broken-heartedly of the death of my young brother, James, who was killed on the Salerno beaches in Italy. Her grief was caused by the fact that she was not sure that James was saved before he died. It was only on her deathbed that she learned that he had accepted the Lord as his Saviour. In the next year I would hear of Mother's death, and then, just a few weeks before the war ended, my brother Fred would also lay down his life on the battlefield in Germany. Several months after I returned to Ireland my father died. It was at times like these that we not only needed a Saviour and friend, but we *had* a Saviour and friend. The Lord's presence became more real and his grace was sufficient for every trial and every need. God supplied «the oil of joy for mourning and the garment of praise for the spirit of heaviness». One verse from the Psalms was such a blessing to me during those times when our loved-ones were taken away—one after the other; when each mail seemed to bring the news of a death in the family. «He shall not be afraid of evil tidings; his heart is fixed, trusting in the Lord.» (Psalm 112:7) I prayed for a fixed heart and I believe the Lord gave me one.

I finally got to the end of my mail with no letter from Cameroon. I had somehow foolishly hoped that I might hear from Elizabeth, although I hadn't written to her and had no reason to expect a letter. But there was a letter from Mac and in it a short note from Elat, signed Elizabeth Hope. It was a formal invitation for me to attend the annual Mission Meeting of the Presbyterian Mission, which lasted for a couple of weeks. The letter was sent by the Mission Meeting secretary, Elizabeth Hope. By no stretch of my imagination could I regard this formal invitation as a love letter, but at least it gave me an opportunity to write to her.

What's the use? There was no postal communication between Spanish Guinea and Cameroon, and only on very rare occasions did a truck pass the frontier. One letter I wrote took six months to reach Elat. But I didn't hesitate to make the trip of more than 350 miles. My personal boy was just as anxious to go to Cameroon as I was. He had never traveled that far in his life, and the fact that we might have to walk most of the trip with him carrying my heavy trunk on his head didn't bother him in the least. The day after I got Mac's letter I packed my trunk and left Acurenan to walk to Elat.

It took two days to reach a large coffee plantation owned by a Spaniard whom I had come to know and who had promised to take me to the coast any time I needed to go and he had a truck going there. We arrived at his place just as he was about to pull out of the yard with a load of coffee for Bata. He immediately offered me a ride and insisted my boy and I eat before we left. Then he put two men off the truck to make room for us! What a provision this was, and how wonderfully God enabled us to reach his place in time to get this ride. He carried us for 90 miles, which would have taken us several days to walk. He left us on the main road to Cameroon, not far from an evangelical church whose pastor invited us to stay with him until we could get a ride to the frontier. He assured me that trucks were passing fairly frequently because it was near to the Christmas season and there was more traffic than usual on the road. This was good news and, sure enough, the following day we got a ride right up to the border of Cameroon.

Our biggest hurdle was to get to Elat from the border. We had another eighty to ninety miles more to travel. The Spanish administrator told me that no traffic had passed for a week from or to Elat, so we started out on foot knowing it would take us four to five days to get there. The Mission Meeting was starting the next day.

Two miles beyond the border (inside Cameroon), we were stopped by Cameroonian gendarmes who were guarding a government post. I had a hard time convincing the sergeant that we were walking to Elat. He had never seen a white man traveling that way. He was suspicious that I was a Spaniard trying to escape the Franco regime in Spanish Guinea. The Spanish colony was not regarded too favorably by the French administrators, who felt that Spain was more on the side of the Germans than the Allies. Then I noticed a telephone pole with a wire stretching back in the direction of Elat. The French administration post was thirty miles further on, and I asked the sergeant if I could speak to the administrator there. He permitted me to do this. When the administrator learned who I was and why I wanted to go to Elat, he said, «Just stay where you are and I'll come and fetch you. In the meantime I will phone Elat and tell them to send someone here to the post to take you on to Elat.

An hour later he turned up in a truck and took us back with him to share a sumptious meal in his home. We had just finished eating when Mac turned up and said in his cheery way, «Hey, we thought you weren't coming, and somebody would have been disappointed if you hadn't made it.» I guess he was referring to Elizabeth, but he never said so and I didn't ask him.

So in record time we had made it to Elat—just three days to cover 350 miles. I hate to think how

111

long it would have taken if the Lord hadn't provided friends and transport along the way. «Surely goodness and mercy shall follow me...»

It was a great relief to hear English again after months of continually listening to Spanish and Okak. The devotional messages, the missionary reports, the workshops, the good times of fellowship were a spiritual stimulation. Everyone made me feel I was part of the Presbyterian Mission.

One thing that bothered me during those two weeks was that I could hardly ever find an opportunity to be alone with Elizabeth. It was impossible to go for a walk, and there were a number of «matchmakers» among the missionary ladies. One evening I did get an opportunity to walk to her house with her and said to her, «Look, it we were back home and not in Africa, we could see each other under normal conditions and date, and get to know one another, but there are no normal circumstances here for dating. Can I ask you a simple question to which I would like a simple answer?»

«Yes, what is your question?»

«Will you marry me?»

«Well,» Elizabeth answered, «your question is simple but the answer is a little more complicated and not easy for me to give you at this moment. I'll think about it. I live with my father, who, as you know is a widower and I don't think he would be happy if I left the Presbyterian Mission and Elat where I was born. Besides, I cannot be replaced in the missionary children's school for two more years. I think it would be better if we waited until our situation is more normal.

«O.K.,» I answered. But I must confess I wondered what a normal situation was like. It seemed like I had been living an abnormal life for a long time. Neither did either of us realize that we would wait

112

for nearly five years before we could both say «Yes» at the altar. Nor for a moment did I think that we would be married in Cincinnati, Ohio, U.S.A. But that is another story.

Not long after I returned to Acurenan from Elat, Miguel, the Acurenan evangelist, came to me and said, «Don Roberto, the people are glad you have come to teach God's Word. They are also glad that you can communicate with some of us in Spanish, but many of our people—especially our older people—do not understand Spanish and they want you to teach them in their own language. If you are not careful, you will rely all the time on your ability to speak Spanish and never learn our Okak language.»

I appreciated Miguel's concern and I knew he was speaking the truth. My mind went back to the situation in Liberia, where the majority of the missionaries had been guilty of not learning the language, and relying all the time upon interpreters.

So I said to him, «Listen, Miguel, I am willing from today not to speak to you again in Spanish if you are willing and all those in the church who speak Spanish are willing to speak to me only in Okak, but remember, I only know a few phrases in your language, and it will be difficult for me to discipline myself not to use Spanish. Also, I will not preach again in the church until I can do it in Okak. Do you agree to help me to do this?»

«Don Roberto, I agree,» he said, «and I will tell all the others to do the same. Also, I will go and find my cousin to work for you; he does not speak a word of Spanish; this will be God's way to help you learn our language.»

I knew Miguel was sincere and I knew he wanted me to learn his language, but I also knew that Miguel wanted me to give his cousin a job. And that is how Mi Tya came to work for me. He was about twenty years old, as strong as an ox, with an engaging smile and a sweet disposition and he was willing to do anything I asked him. For a dollar a week and his food, where could I get a better all round worker?

My life was very simple. I could have easily made what meals I ate, but Mi Tya insisted on cooking my meals. He had not the foggiest idea how to cook; in fact, I had to teach him how. But his greatest asset was his ignorance of Spanish. Every day, three hours in the morning and three hours in the afternoon for nearly nine months, I studied Bulu and Okak. I sat on one side of the table with my Bulu grammar, dictionary, Bible and hymnbook and read Bulu while Mi Tya told me how to pronounce certain words in Okak that were different from Bulu. I read through the Gospels several times as I found it easier than the Epistles. Then I read through the *Pilgrim's Progress* as well as memorizing a number of the Bulu hymns we sang in church every day. Then I began to read the Bulu literature, changing all the Bulu words into Okak that were not the same in Bulu and, slowly but surely, I began to figure out the difference in the nuances of words in both languages, as well as changes in the grammar.

At the end of nine months I memorized a short gospel message and a Bible study and preached them in the church. Everyone in the church applauded me! It had been one of the hardest things I had ever done in my life, not to speak in church when I could have done it in Spanish. But I was determined to learn Okak and I thank God He enabled me to do it. During the last eighteen months I spent in Spanish Guinea, I could speak, preach and teach God's Word fairly easily in Okak. What a joy and thrill it was to be able to do this.

I had some very strange experiences during the three years I lived among the Okak people. In many ways their culture was the same as that of the Liberian bush people, but in other ways they were different. One thing they did share in common was their fear of evil spirits, and their superstitious customs were usually related to witchcraft and idolatrous worship. They were animists and pantheists, and firmly believed that spirits lived everywhere; in trees, stones, rivers and so forth.

I wasn't long in Africa until I realized that this fear of evil spirits was something very real to them. I never joked or teased them about this or treated the subject lightly. Witchcraft, as practiced in Africa, is almost always associated with cruelty as well as fear. The Psalmist said, «For the dark places of the earth are full of the habitations of cruelty.» (Psalm 74:20) This is certainly true of many parts of pagan Africa, where spiritual darkness is intense and the people «who through fear of death were all their lifetime subject to bondage.» (Hebrews 2:14)

When I first arrived in Acurenan and was welcomed by several hundred believers, I noticed among them a woman, who every time she approached me, would shake her head violently from side to side, and when she tried to speak she was tongue-tied. I saw her several times during that weekend, standing at a distance from the church, and when I tried to go near her she shook her head and backed away. I spoke to Melo, the church elder, about her and he said rather reluctantly (because it was obvious he did not wish to talk about her), «Don Roberto, when Mr. Thorne first came to Acurenan that woman believed. Ma Mondo (Emma) taught her how to read God's Word. She was received into the church and was baptisted. After her baptism she immediately left the church and returned to her former life of worshipping evil spirits. She lost her power of speech and now she is crazy.»

«Why don't we pray for her? I asked him, and recounted my experience in Liberia with Goa the soldier.

Melo listened intently and then said, «Well, maybe God will deliver her if we pray like that.»

So Melo's wife persuaded this woman to come to church one day so we could pray for her. I called Miguel and Melo and we tried to pray for her. But as soon as Melo started to pray the poor woman let out a guttural scream and rushed out of the church. I never saw her again until I was leaving Acurenan to return to Ireland, and she came along with others to say goodbye to Emma and me. Melo and I tried again to pray with her for deliverance from her demon possession, but we had the same reaction from her. She fled down the road screaming and that was the last we saw of her. I was troubled and saddened because, for some reason, we did not seem to have the faith to believe for her deliverance and felt very much like the disciples of Jesus, when they too, were helpless before the demon-possessed boy and Jesus told them, «This kind goeth not out but by prayer and fasting.» (Matthew 17:21)

But God did give us many wonderful answers to prayer. Soon after my sister returned from furlough and arrived at Acurenan, I had to go to Bata to register her with the police in order to obtain a ration card. There were some European canned foods that occasionally arrived from Spain, but they were strictly rationed among the white people. We lived almost entirely off the land.

On the way down to Bata I felt somewhat apprehensive about going to the chief of police (who took care of immigration in Rio Muni), simply because I had entered the country eighteen months before without asking anyone's permission to do so. Now I was going for the first time, at the insistence of the Acurenan administrator, to report to the police for both my sister and myself. The policy the missionaries had used in the past was, «If you ask permission, they are often obliged to say no, even if they don't wish to say so. If you don't ask permission, nine times out of ten they won't even bother you.» On one occasion, for example, when I went to the Acurenan administrator to ask him for a small favor in regard to the church, he looked at me coldly and said, «Sir, I don't even know you have a church here.» The church—which held 300 people—was built along the motor road, five hundred yards from his office!

I had been informed by Mr. McNeill that the new chief of police, whom I had never met and who had been recently installed in Bata, was bitterly opposed to evangelical work. So I wasn't looking forward to meeting him. I wouldn't have gone if the Acurenan administrator, who was also opposed to evangelical work, had not insisted on my doing so. All the way to the coast I kept reminding the Lord that I was His ambassador in Spanish Guinea, even though the Spanish authorities did not regard us as such! So I prayed for wisdom and claimed God's promise in James 1:5, «If any of you lack wisdom, let him ask of God who giveth to all men liberally and upbraideth not, and it shall be given him.» I was hoping that I would not have the same experience I had had with the police in Lagos.

Mr. McNeill was out of the country, and how I wished he were there to go with me. He had had years of dealing with difficult officials in Bata, but they all respected him highly. He was not there, however, and I reminded myself that the Lord was there and He could go before and make the crooked paths straight. He surely did, beyond what I had hoped and prayed for.

117

However, I must confess, as I entered the Chief of Police office I felt nervous. He came in and sat behind his desk and looked at me without a word of greeting and then in a curt, businesslike manner he said, «What can I do for you?» When I informed him of the purpose of my visit he raised his eyebrows in astonishment and asked me, «How did you come into this country, and what are you doing here?» I told him I had come from Liberia at the request of my mission to join my sister, who had already lived in the country for seven years. This information astonished him still more and he asked me, «Are you also a missionary?»

I said to him, «Yes, sir, I am a missionary.»

«Will you kindly tell me what is a missionary and what is he doing in Spanish Guinea?» he asked me.

I don't believe he had ever met a missionary apart from the Catholic priests and he was sincere in asking me this question. But I also knew that this man sitting before me had the authority to put Emma and me out of the country with a stroke of his pen. So like Nehemiah when he stood before the king with troubled countenance, (Nehemiah 2:4, 5) I, too, prayed to the God of heaven for wisdom how to answer this question, and the Lord answered my prayer in a very unusual way. I told him what I had been doing and how long I had been in the country.

«Show me your passport,» he commanded me.

I handed it to him. He opened it and his eyes seemed to open wider and for what seemed an eternity he examined my passport.

«What is the matter?» I wondered. «Has he seen that bogus Spanish visa that caused me so much trouble in Lagos?»

But it wasn't the passport or the visa he was examining. It was a bunch of foreign stamps I had

118

absent-mindedly put in my passport some months before.

«Are you a stamp collector?» he asked me.

«No, sir, I am not.»

«Then why are you saving these stamps?» he asked.

«Oh, to give to my friends,» I answered.

He leaned across his desk, and for the first time he smiled at me. Would you consider me as one of your friends?» he asked.

One of his friends! I could scarcely believe what I heard or what was happening. He had already scooped up the stamps and was carefully examining them and at the same time pushed my passport back to me across his desk. Then he looked up and said, «Would you care to see my stamp collection?»

«I would be delighted,» I told him.

He left his office and went across the road to his home. While he was gone I called his secretary, who was a Bulu fellow and a believer and member of the Presbyterian church in Cameroon, and said to him, «Hey, brother, stamp my passport and my sister's; the chief of police wants me to be his friend.» He grinned at me as he had heard the whole conversation and he duly stamped our passports. The police chiefs were frequently changed in Spanish Guinea and I thought they might not all be stamp collectors!

When he returned with his stamp albums I casually asked him if he wished to check our passports and he said, «No, no, my clerk will do that for you if you wish.»

For the next thirty minutes I shared his enthusiasm for stamp collecting. I left his office «walking on air.» Every time I had occasion to go to Bata I took him more stamps, just to solidify our friendship. How true the Scripture that says, «The king's heart is in the hand of the Lord, like the rivers of water; he turneth it whithersoever he will.» (Proverbs 21:1)

I returned to Acurenan on the truck that carried our mail. When this was given to us I noticed a cable among the letters. It was from Belfast and stated simply, «Mother dead letter following.» This sudden news of her death was a tremendous shock to Emma who had left Mother a few months before in apparent good health. It was nearly five years since I had seen her and I had had a premonition that I wouldn't see her again on earth. The news of her death brought heaven a little closer to us.

Emma was anxious to go down to the Kogo area where several WEC churches were located. She had been away from the field for nearly two years and was anxious to see the believers again, most of whom she had personally led to Christ. It was to be our first and last trek together through southern Spanish Guinea, and just writing about it brings back many wonderful and precious memories. I had already made several trips there for communion services, but this was a very exciting time for the Kogo believers to see us together as brother and sister, sharing their lives and ministering the Word of God to them.

It took us two weeks of walking to reach the Kogo beach. The news of our coming was relayed from village to village by native drummers, so that when we arrived where a church was located the congregation was already waiting for us. We spent three weeks in the area gossiping the gospel all day long and late into the night. It was hot and humid. Kogo is almost on the equator.

I remember one afternoon when I was resting—it was stiffling hot. One of my Spanish friends told me once, «Señor, only dogs and missionaries walk between noon and three.» Well, it was that kind of day. Miguel, along with his brother Henrique—who was also an evangelist—came to me and said, «Don Roberto, there is a man outside the house who wishes to speak to you. He wishes to confess Christ as his Saviour.»

I went outside and there stood before me a giant of a man. He must have been six feet six inches tall, with broad shoulders and muscles rippling all over his body. He could have entered the Mr. Universe contest, and probably won it. I asked him why he wanted to see me, and he answered that he wished to be delivered from his fetishes and his witchcraft. It was always good news to hear these words, and we had heard them a number of times. In fact, when an Okak man or woman professed faith in Christ they were always asked, «Do you have any fetishes; do you have any taboos?» A taboo usually consisted of a prohibition by a witch doctor or by the tribe that a person could not eat certain foods, or could not do certain things or visit certain places.

There were all kinds of taboos and under no condition would a person break the taboo for fear of annoying the evil spirits, which could cause him to suffer physically or even suffer death. They were too scared of dying. So when the answer was in the affirmative, they were invariably asked by the believers to break the taboo by eating the forbidden food as a proof of their sincerity in believing in Christ. I have seen them tremblingly put a banana or fish to their mouth—which for years had been taboo for them—and eat it, while their pagan friends stood around horrified, expecting the person to drop dead. Thank God none of them ever did! Breaking a taboo was no joke, and we never treated it lightly but as something satanic which only the power of Christ could break. He breaks the power of canceled sin; He sets the prisoner free.

So I asked the big man if he had any taboos.

No he hadn't. «What, then, are your fetishes?» He told me what they were. Many of the Okak people worshiped the spirits of their forefathers. Sometimes they kept the skulls of their forefathers, believing that the spirits of their forebears lived in their skulls. This man had four skulls back in his house in the forest, and it was these that he wished to get rid of. Would we go and destroy them for him.

Henrique and Miguel accompanied me, and all four of us returned to the man's house, deep in the forest. Why did they always keep these fetishes and perform their idolatrous rituals deep in the forest? Because men love darkness better than light because their deeds are evil. Jesus said this in John 3:19. He kept his skulls in a small, coffin-like basket under his bed. We took them back in their basket to where Emma and I were staying. As we walked back through the bush with Miguel carrying the basket on his head, men, women and children who met us took one glance at the basket and dived off the path into the bush. They apparently knew what was inside and were scared, not of the skulls but of the spirits. I asked Emma what we should do with them and she told me, «You can't bury them, because someone else might dig them up and add them to his collection! Ask Henrique, he will know what to do with them.»

A large crowd of unbelievers as well as Christians had gathered in the village. This man was apparently well known in the region and everyone wondered what he was going to do with his fetishes. Henrique suggested that we throw them into the Kogo River. It was wide and deep and the pagan people would not dare to try to recuperate them for fear of offending the river spirits.

So we all marched down to the river. I spoke to them of God's power to destroy sin through the death of Christ on the cross, emphasizing that Christ had come to destroy the works of the devil. (I John 3:8) A number of the believers gave testimonies as to how God had freed them from taboos and superstitious practices. Then Henrique spoke to the crowd and said to them, «Don Roberto and I are going to throw this basket of skulls into the river because this is what our friend wishes.» So he and I took the basket and flung it as far as we could out into the river.

The basket must have weighed about fifteen pounds, and I thought it would sink immediately, but it didn't and continued to float for quite a while and even began to drift back towards us where we stood on the bank. The pagan people watched, fascinated, and many of them believed that the river spirits were holding it up. I told Henrique to pray that it would sink, and as he prayed I kept watching it. Suddenly with a gurgle it disappeared to the bottom of the river.

When Henrique opened his eyes and saw that the basket had disappeared he turned to the big man and asked him, «Where are your fetishes?»

«Out there,» he answered, pointing native fashion with his lips protruding.

«Can you see them?»

«No.»

«Why not?»

«Because the water has covered them.»

«Can you recover them?»

«No. They are gone forever; the water has covered them.»

Then Henrique said to him, addressing himself at the same time to all who were standing at the river, «Listen, my brother. As the waters have covered your fetishes, so the blood of Jesus Christ has covered your sins. Pray.»

Then the man prayed this simple prayer and it was the first time he had ever prayed publicly. He didn't close his eyes but simply looked up to the sky and prayed:

A Tata Zambe m'ave wo akeva,
Amu me nto nti, nya ntian.

«O Lord God I give you thanks, because I am free, truly free.»

When I heard him pray that prayer, I thought of two things: John Bunyan's famous pilgrim arriving at the foot of the cross and lifting up his eyes to where his sins had been placed upon Christ, and the burden of his sins rolling off his shoulders and into the empty tomb, never to be carried again. And secondly, the words of Jesus came to my mind, «If therefore the Son shall make you free, you shall be free indeed.» (John 8:36)

Just to hear that pagan man pray that prayer was worth all the sweat and toil and the long days of walking through the forest to the Kogo beach. «O Lord God I give thee thanks because I am free, truly free.» Free from the fear and bondage of sin to serve the living and true God. What a joy and privilege to share this good news with men and women everywhere, especially in the dark places of the earth which are full of the habitations of cruelty.

Can we whose souls are lighted, with
wisdom from on high
Can we to men benighted, the
lamp of life deny?

I did not know that this would be the last long gospel trek I would make in the African bush. I'm glad I didn't because I know it would have troubled me.

Emma and I returned to Acurenan after spending seven weeks in the bush. Many had made professions of faith in Christ; the believers were encouraged and strengthened in the Lord; in two places they wanted to build churches. God supplied our needs in many wonderful ways.

Henrique, the evangelist, was not only a good preacher and fisher of men but also a good fisher of fish! He was a skilled fisherman and whenever he accompanied us on a gospel trek, he always took along his wide, round fishing net. Fish abound in African rivers, and in no time at all, Henrique could catch enough fish to feed our whole company. When he made an extra large catch he would smoke what wasn't eaten, so we ate smoked fish for days even when we were far from the big river. It sometimes got monotonous, however, to eat smoked fish day after day. One day I jokingly said to Henrique, «Say, brother, do you think you could catch some meat with your net instead of fish?»

Henrique laughed and said to me, «Don Roberto, when we get to the beach in a day or two, I will catch you meat that you have never tasted in your life.»

Sure enough, a few days later Henrique came to us with a huge turtle he had caught on the beach. It was quickly prepared and cooked while someone went off into the bush to find mushrooms. These were found and cooked with the turtle steaks. They were delicious. We ate that meal in September of 1945.

In December 1974 nearly thirty years later, Betty and I were en route to Guatemala where I had been invited by the Central American Mission to teach in the Guatemala Bible Institute in Chimaltenango. In the spring of 1974 we had done a refresher course in Spanish at the Spanish Language Institute in San José, Costa Rica. While there we met a fine couple—graduates of Columbia Bible College—who worked in Acapulco, Mexico, and who were in the same class with me. Richard and Anita Dye had invited us to visit them in the famous Acapulco, so on the way through Mexico we spent a long weekend with them.

Anita is an excellent cook and prepared several delicious Mexican dishes for us. One evening when we came to the table for supper, Anita said, «Bob and Betty, I am going to serve you meat that I know you have never tasted in your life, and we want you to guess what it is.»

Where had I heard those words before? In a flash my mind went back to the Kogo beach and Henrique and the turtle steaks. I tasted the meat and said, «Oh, yes, I have tasted this before. It's turtle steak; I have eaten it in Africa.» And I told the Dyes about our trip to Kogo.

When the Lord Jesus sent out His disciples to preach the gospel, He exhorted them to take only the absolute essentials for living. They were not to burden themselves with non-essentials. In some measure I believe I learned this lesson in Africa. It was not because we didn't have money; we did, but there was not much to buy in wartime Africa, at least not where we lived. On those gospel treks in Spanish Guinea we were given food and shelter freely. I was always amazed at the generosity of our African brothers and sisters in Christ. Part of their culture? Perhaps. But often they were desperately poor and yet out of their poverty they gave and gave, and often I was put to shame. This is why I can understand what Paul wrote about the Macedonian churches.

Moreover, brethren, we made known to you the grace of God bestowed on the churches of Macedonia,

How that in a great trial of affliction the abundance of their joy and their deep poverty abounded unto the riches of their liberality.

For to their power I bear witness, yea, beyond their power they were willing of themselves,

Beseeching us with much entreaty that we would receive the gift.

(II Corinthians 8:1-4)

We saw this «grace of giving» demonstrated over and over by our African brethren. We tried to return their kindness by sharing the gospel with them, seeking to alleviate their physical suffering, rejoicing with those that rejoiced and weeping with those that wept. We saw much of the Lord's working in their lives that caused us to rejoice and often we had experiences that truly made us weep.

One of the things at that time in Equatorial Guinea that made us weep, perhaps more than anything else, was the high mortality among little children. I never got used to seeing a child playing on the mission compound, full of fun and life, and then sometimes a few days later I would be asked to bury it. This happened over and over again. In fact, we had a small, children's cemetery on the mission compound. There was a reason why the church members brought their children to be buried on the compound, a horrible reason.

Among the Okak people existed a secret society called the BURU. The BURU performed evil initiation rituals and practiced the eating of human flesh. This did not mean that they warred among themselves and ate their enemies, as was practised in some of the South Sea Islands. It was part of their superstitious worship of spirits. At certain times of the year the society would meet deep in the forest after having exhumed a recently buried body. Parts of the deceased person would be smoked and dried and eaten in a ritual too horrible to describe. One of our converts was a former kind of high priest or witch-doctor in this society, and it was he who told me part of their ritualistic worship, only part of it. A man who was a hunter, for example, would eat the trigger finger of a famous dead hunter in order to have success in his hunting. Women would participate hoping to bear children. Some would participate in order to put taboos on their enemies.

Paul wrote to the Ephesians and said, «For it is a shame to speak of those things which are done among them in secret.» (Ephesians 5:12) I simply mention some of these things in passing to explain why the Christian Okaks brought their dead to be buried on the mission compound rather than in a grave near to their villages, in case the little bodies of their children should be exhumed and eaten.

A woman came one day to my sister Emma and sat on the ground in front of her and began to moan and sway back and forth, repeating over and over, «One, two, three, four, five, six, seven, all dead and eaten.» Whether this was true or not, I do not know, but she believed it was true—and it probably was.

So not once, but often, we wept with them when we buried their children. I do not have any reason to believe that the mortality rate among children in Equatorial Guinea is any less today than it was thirty-five years ago when we were there.

In the spring of 1945 a new administrator arrived in Acurenan. He had served in the Spanish Blue Division that fought against the Russians and had lost the fingers of one hand. He was a bitter man and a professed agnostic, as well as hating the British. After he settled into the government post I went to see him to pay my respects. How thankful I was that Emma and I now had official permission to work in the country, thanks to my friendship with the chief of police in Bata. The first question this new administrator asked me was, «Do you and your sister have official permission to reside in this country?» I assured him we did have permission. Then he called his servant to bring wine. I told him politely that it was against the principles and practices of my Mission to drink wine, but I would be happy to drink a lemonade with him!

«What do you mean, you don't drink wine? Don't you evangelicals celebrate the Lord's supper, holy communion?» he asked me.

«Yes, some do,» I told him. «But we evangelicals do not believe that the bread and wine can be changed into the body and blood of the Saviour,» I added.

He filled a glass and held it up in front of me, and said with a mocking sneer on his face, «I toast the blood of Christ.»

«Sir,» I said to him quietly and respectfully, «Some day you will stand before Christ and He will judge you for this blasphemy you have just uttered.»

He was livid with rage and said to me between clenched teeth, «You may leave my house, sir.» I left, glad to be out of his presence.

There were about twenty Spanish people, single men and some families, living in Acurenan. They were mostly merchants and government officials. We had a very good relationship with all of them. I had extracted teeth for some of them, including the wife of the former administrator, who was a sergeant and who had been replaced by the present administrator. I had also assisted at the birth of the baby of a Spanish couple who lived not far from our house, so we had many friends among the white colony in Acurenan.

When the news leaked out of my interview with the captain and our «quarrel», a number of our

Spanish friends came to our house to apologize for him. They felt angry about it.

Among them, and probably the most friendly of all, was a merchant by the name of Antonio Tejera, whose store was right opposite our church on the other side of the motor road. Several days after the episode with the captain, Antonio called me over to his house and said to me, «Don Roberto, I want to warn you about the administrator. He has sworn to have you and your sister deported from the colony. The first word that you say that might be construed as a criticism of Spain or Franco, or the government here, then you will be expelled.» I thanked him for his confidence and assured him that we would be more than careful.

Every afternoon at five we had a service in the church. The Acurenan church had an open space in place of a door, and the windows were also just open spaces. People often stood outside the door or windows when they were afraid to come into the church. It was very easy for Antonio Tejera to listen to the messages as he sat outside his store. He often did.

After Antonio's warning I began to notice that the captain came almost every afternoon with the pretext of visiting Antonio. He and his servant, an Okak fellow, stayed outside Antonio's store and listened to everything I preached from the pulpit. This continued for two weeks and was, of course, noticed by everyone, including Antonio, who wasn't bluffed at all by the captain's pretended friendliness to him.

Melo came to me one day and said, «Don Roberto, we are all afraid that the administrator is going to send you and Ma Mondo out of the country. Everyone in Acurenan knows he hates you and God's work. I would like to suggest that we meet every day to pray that God will not permit this to happen.» So several of us did meet to ask God to expel the captain and not us, and this is exactly what happened. We never did learn the details, but apparently he had done something to annoy his superior in Bata and he was sent back to Spain in disgrace. Praise the Lord!

The morning the captain left Acurenan the school-children and others living on the mission campus lined up along the read to give him the fascist salute, which they were obliged to do when a government official passed in his car. As he passed they all obediently stretched out their arms to salute him. I couldn't help smiling at what happened next. As the captain's pickup disappeared down the road everyone waved him goodbye. Melo came running across the campus and said to me, «Don Roberto, God has answered our prayers. He has gone. They come and they go, but God's work goes on forever.»

I have thought of Melo's words during the past ten years when Spanish Guinea has suffered terror and bloodshed at the hands of one of the cruelest dictators the African continent has known, and I refer to Ngueme Macias, who was recently overthrown in a military coup and executed. Jesus said, «I will build my church and the gates of hell shall not prevail against it.» (Matthew 16:18)

Five years had passed since I arrived in Africa. The war had come to an end in Europe but was still being fought in the Far East. I began to make plans to return to Ireland. I hadn't heard from Elizabeth for eighteen months. I knew she had returned to the States, but I had no idea how to get in touch with her. I hadn't had much time to think about her in the last year and had committed my future and hers to the Lord and left it at that.

There was one corner of the colony that I wanted to visit before I left the country. It had not been visited, as far as I knew, by any evangelicals. Miguel and Mi Tya accompanied me and we spent five days walking through this part, preaching the gospel. On our way back to Acurenan I stopped at a coffee plantation owned by a Spaniard. The first thing he said to me was, «The war is over; the Americans have dropped an atomic bomb on Nagasaki and on Hiroshima, and Japan has surrendered. All is over.»

When I got back to Acurenan, I was informed by Mr. Thorne, who had returned to Spanish Guinea just a few months before, that his wife was ill and had to return to England and would I be willing to take her home. I was willing, of course, to do this, but her going made it impossible for my sister to stay on alone with Mr. Thorne. So Emma was also obliged to return to Ireland. I felt I should tell Mr. Thorne that I was seriously thinking of returning to Bible college for further study.

«How long do you think you will study?» he asked me.

«Possibly two years,» I told him, «maybe five.»

«Well, Robert,» he said, «I don't believe you will ever be back again in Spanish Guinea.» I guess his words were prophetic because I never did get back to Africa.

Mr. and Mrs. Frank Chapman and another single girl, all Canadian WECers, along with Emma, labored in Spanish Guinea until the middle of the sixties. Mrs. Thorne died in England and Mr. Thorne retired to Australia, where he died. Spanish Guinea gained its independence from Spain in 1968, and was taken over by Ngueme Macias, a ruthless dictator. All missionaries were expelled in 1968, both Catholic and Protestant. The following information is taken from *OPERATION WORLD*, by Patrick Johnstone, research editor for the Worldwide Evangelization Crusade. It was written before the overthrow of Ngueme Macias in 1979.

EQUATORIAL AFRICA

BACKGROUND

Area: 28,000 kilometers—small enclave, Rio Muni, on the African mainland and a 2,000 sq. km. island, Fernando Po (now called Ngueme Macias) in the Gulf of Guinea.

Population: 300,000 (25 % on Fernando Po) a further 100,000, at least, have fled for refuge in the surrounding Cameroon and Gabon.

Economy: Almost total collapse with the flight of all Europeans and the murder of virtually all the educated and skilled people.

Politics: Independent of Spain since 1968. A coup in 1969 brought the present President Ngueme Macias to power. The dictator has turned the country into a virtual concentration camp, murdered all the educated and all likely to oppose him, and imposed a Marxist style government.

Religion: *Attitude of government*—militant atheism and all religions ruthlessly supressed. The only worship permitted is that given to the President.
African traditionals 8 %.
Roman Catholics 88 %—due to the assiduous efforts of Roman Catholic missionaries to baptise as many as possible. Now all Roman Catholic churches closed or converted to other uses and the last priests believed to be in prison.
Protestants 3.5 % though now probably less.
Two denominations: Presbyterian 9,000 community (Rio Muni) and Methodists, 800 (Fernando Po)
Evangelicals 2 %.

1) *The unfortunate people have suffered intensely.* May this turn many to the Lord Jesus for comfort. Pray for an end to this terrible regime.

2) *The persecution of these believers has rarely been exceeded anywhere in Africa.* Many believers have lost their lives, others are forced into slavery. It is now illegal to hold church meetings, give money to a church or minister,

associate with a pastor, conduct Christian funerals or be baptised without government permission. How many dare apply? Pray for the believers. There are some reports that the believers still continue to witness where possible.

3) *It is reported that the Presbyterians and Methodists were ordered to worship the President at the beginning of every service.* Pray that the believers will not compromise. Many of the believers in the south of the country are the fruit of the years of WEC missionaries who worked there. These believers joined up with the Presbyterians when all missionaries were expelled in 1968.

Such is the report on Equatorial Guinea written by Patrick Johnstone a few years ago. Since the overthrow of the dictator Ngueme Macias, word is coming out of Equatorial Guinea at this point in time (February 1980), that the new government is encouraging its citizens who fled the country to return. Christians and pastors from Spanish Guinea who fled to Cameroon are free to return to their homeland. This is certainly a wonderful answer to prayer, and nothing would please the writer more than to be able to return to Equatorial Africa to share once again in their joys and sorrows. If we cannot return, we shall always be grateful to God that He permitted us to spend a few years at least in this small corner of His vineyard on the African continent.

> After this I beheld, and lo, a great multitude which no man could number, and people and tongues, stood before the throne and before the Lamb, clothed with white robes, and palms in their hands;
>
> And they cried, saying, Salvation to our God which sitteth upon the throne and unto the Lamb...
>
> And one of the elders answered unto me, saying, What are these which are arrayed in white robes, and whence cometh they?
>
> And I said unto him, Sir, thou knowest. And he said unto me, These are they that came out of great tribulation and have washed their robes and made them white in the blood of the lamb.

Therefore are they before the throne of God and serve him day and night in his temple, and he that sitteth on the throne shall dwell with them.

They shall hunger no more, neither thirst any more, neither shall the sun light on them nor any heat,

For the Lamb which is in the midst of the throne shall feed them and God shall wipe away all tears from their eyes.

(Revelation 7:9-17)

I often wonder when I read this passage how many of our Okak brothers and sisters will be among this special group of martyrs as they stand before the throne of God and of the Lamb? Undoubtedly many, because they loved not their lives unto death.

CHAPTER 7

Go West Young Man

It was with mixed feelings that I said goodbye to the believers in Acurenan and headed once more for Cameroon, en route to Ireland and home. It never entered my mind for a moment that I would not return to Africa. For three years I had prayed that God would make it possible for me to get the kind of theological education I felt I needed in order to return to Africa and engage in a Bible school ministry.

A spirit of nationalism was manifest everywhere in Africa and it was evident that the French, Spanish, Belgian, British and Portuguese colonies were not only going to demand independence from the colonial powers but fight for it, if need be. The day was coming, and coming fast, when the role of the foreign missionary would no longer be that of evangelist, church planter, administrator, but rather as counselor and inspirer of his African colleagues. He would not only have to be willing to work *with*, but if needs be, *under* the African. What better way to accomplish this than to train Africans to evangelize Africans. This would be one field in which the foreign missionary could excel.

Thinking of all this made me more determined than ever that I would go back to Bible college and seminary and complete my Bible education which was lacking. In thinking of this, I turned my eyes to the west - to the United States - where I felt I could get the kind of sound theological education I wanted.

The journey back to England was almost as long as the one out to Africa in 1940. The ship stopped at every West African port to pick up more and more passengers. There were hundreds of people trying to get back to Britain and our ship was crowded and uncomfortable. Passengers bunked down wherever they could find a comfortable spot on the ship.

As we got closer to England it became colder. Most of us were wearing light tropical clothes and felt the cold intensely. «When I get to Liverpool,» I thought, «I'll buy a heavy suit, a sweater and an overcoat.» But when I got ashore and entered the first clothing store I discovered that I couldn't buy anything without clothing coupons issued by the government. The lady in the store told me where to go to get a ration book, but I had to wait two days before I could obtain one.

I was staying again at Emmanuel Bible College in Birkenhead and, when the students learned that I didn't have coupons to buy needed clothing, several of them loaned me enough to buy what I needed. I returned the coupons later because in post-war Britain coupons were almost as precious as money, for without them, money had little value. There were other restrictions in Britain that I was to learn about later.

I arrived back in Belfast three days before Christmas after an absence of six years. Much of the center of the city had been demolished by the air raids. Our two shops and dwelling houses had disappeared completely. Mother, Fred and James were also gone, and my father, who had received the Lord as his Saviour after Mother's death, was dying and died six months later. The hymn writer was right when he wrote, «Change and decay in all around I see...» The war had affected almost every family in Britain one way or another.

More than ever I turned my eyes to the west and the possibility of seeing Elizabeth again. We had lost touch with each other, not having written to each other for nearly two years. I was not sure she was still in the States and thought it most likely that she had returned to Cameroon. I did not know a single person in the United States to whom I could write. So I tried to forget her, but this was not easy. I had written to Columbia Bible College, as I had gotten to know about this school through Elizabeth and her father. I was accepted to enter in the fall term of 1946. Perhaps I might learn something about her there at the CBC Alumni office. The College does try to keep in touch with the movements of its alumni, and might possibly know where she was, but it seemed like it would be a miracle for us to meet in the States.

It was one thing to be accepted as a student at Columbia Bible College; it was another thing to get there. First of all, I had to go to London and talk with the WEC leadership about my furlough plans. I asked for a leave of absence for two years, possibly five. My request was refused, so I had no alternative but to resign from the WEC after being part of the Crusade for nearly ten interesting and happy years. I had enjoyed the pioneering aspect and the faith emphasis of the mission and I had learned many lessons working under its auspices. In many ways I was sorry the Lord did not lead me back into the WEC, but He had other plans for me that I had not yet dreamed of.

Immediately after I got back from London I began to make preparations for the United States. During my five years in Africa I had saved about $1500 because we spent very little money in Africa. The WEC continued to send me an allowance for six months after my resignation, which I appreciated. Through gifts from friends and speaking in meetings I added another five hundred dollars to my savings. I figured I had enough money to get to Columbia and pay my first year's room and board, which came to about $1,000. «All I have to do now,» I thought, «is to get a visa, buy a boat ticket to New York and a bus ticket to Columbia.»

In post-war Britain, however, life was not as simple and normal as that. First of all, I was informed by the shipping agencies that thousands of G.I. brides from all over Europe were wanting to join their husbands and these were getting priority over all others. Very few people were flying and in order to book a flight to the States, I had to produce a visa from the U.S. consulate. When I went to the consulate for a visa, I was informed I couldn't get one unless I had a flight assured. It was a vicious circle.

Finally TWA offered me a flight to New York and it looked like my problem was solved about getting a visa, but it wasn't. There was one more hurdle. Unless I could find some one to sponsor me in the U.S., or could give proof that I could support myself for at least a year, I couldn't obtain a visa. «But

I will have $1500,» I told the consul. «This is enough for one year's college expenses.» Wonderful days when you could go to college for a year for $1500, all needs met!

«No, it is not enough,» he told me. «You will have to have this money transferred to the States and at the moment the Bank of England will not permit it. Until you can give me assurance that your money has been transferred to the USA, I cannot issue you a visa. Sorry.»

What to do? I didn't know what to do or how to get around this obstacle. «Lord,» I prayed, «I don't know how You are going to do it, but I know and believe that You can even change the immigration laws, if needs be, to get me into the United States.»

My brother-in-law and sister lived in Glasgow, Scotland. Ernie was pastor of a Church of the Nazarene. They invited me to visit them so, more for a change of scenery than anything else, I went over to Glasgow. My visit corresponded with the annual convention of the British Nazarene churches which was being convened in Glasgow and I was invited to the meetings. Most of the meetings were for discussing the business and expansion of the denomination. I found them pretty boring for the most part, until one afternoon my attention was aroused when one of the pastors said, «There it is, brethren, we have $1500 in the USA but because of the Bank of England restrictions we cannot get the money transferred, and we need it. Pray that God will show us how to solve this problem.»

Immediately after the meeting I went to this pastor and told him, «Brother, I have the solution to your problem; in fact, I *am* the solution!» I then told him of my problem to get my money transferred to the States, and I said to him, «If you can give me the assurance that I can collect your money in the

141

States, I will give you a check for the amount right now.» He was delighted. A week later he was in Belfast and went with me to the American consul and assured him that the Church of the Nazarene in the United States would be willing, officially, to sponsor me in the States. That was all the consul wished to know and immediately issued me a student visa.

So my casual visit to Glasgow was directly in the will of God to make it possible for me to go to the USA and it solved two problems at the same time. «His ways are not our ways, neither His thoughts our thoughts.» (Isaiah 55:8)

When I left the consulate that afternoon I experienced the same feeling of elation that I had had when I left the censor's office in London six years before. I kept saying to myself, «Go west, young man, you are on your way to the United States.»

It was June 1946. My father had gone to be with Christ; I had no family ties; I was leaving on August 3. I was so excited and challenged about going back to study and about the new life that would be mine in the U.S. that I could hardly sleep at nights thinking about it all. If only I knew how to get in touch with Elizabeth, it would be perfect, but I didn't know how, and that was the only shade of grey in the whole beautiful picture.

Three days before I left Belfast for New York I received a package in the mail. It was from the Presbyterian Mission in New York City. It was a book that Elizabeth had promised to send me two years before. She had given instructions in the New York office to have the book sent to me, but her request had been overlooked. Inside the book was a little note from her explaining why the book had not been sent, saying she was sending it to Belfast hoping I would find it when I got back from Africa. She added, «I shall be returning to Cameroon in two weeks' time.»

I could scarcely believe it. I read the note several times. «So she is actually in New York,» I thought, «and I will be there myself on Sunday morning.» It seemed too good to be true. Is this just a coincidence, or is it the Lord who is intervening in our lives? I wanted to believe with all my heart that it was the Lord who was guiding us so wonderfully and I thought of the experience of Abraham's servant when he was sent by Abraham to look for a bride for Isaac. When he had found her, his testimony was, «I being in the way, the Lord led me to the house of my master's brethren.» (Genesis 24:27) I committed it to the Lord and I knew that He would lead us just as perfectly as He had led Eliezer.

On Sunday afternoon I arrived in New York City and stayed in the Sudan Interior Mission headquarters. I immediately phoned Kennedy House, owned by the Presbyterian Mission, and used for missionary accommodation. When I asked if I could speak with Elizabeth Hope I was told she had just left a few minutes before to go to a conference center in Chautaugua, New York.

«Where is Chautaugua?» I asked. «Is it far from here?»

«Oh, yes, it is a long way from New York City,» they informed me.

«Can you give me her phone number?» I asked.

«Sorry, I don't believe you could reach her by phone. It is a conference center and I have no idea where she would be staying.»

To say I was disappointed would be putting it mildly. I sat for some time wondering about it all. Is it possible that after two years of traveling several thousand miles that we should miss each other like this by a few minutes? Well, forget about it; see New York and then take a bus to Columbia and get down there early to get ready for the opening of school.

I don't know how Herb and Marion Congo, WEC missionaries with whom I had worked at Gaypeter station in Liberia, knew that I was at the SIM headquarters. They phoned me that same evening and invited me to join them at a conference center near Albany, N.Y. I was delighted to know they were in the States and left the next morning to join them at Round Lake conference. They insisted on my going with them to Ottawa, and later to the WEC headquarters in Toronto. I had found some friends on the North American continent.

At the end of August I boarded a Greyhound bus for New York and Columbia, stopping again at the SIM mission house in New York. I remembered Elizabeth had said she was leaving for Cameroon in two weeks. She had probably gone. Might as well try to forget about her. Easier said than done. I picked up the phone and called Kennedy House and asked if I could speak to Elizabeth Hope.

«Just a minute,» the voice said, «and I'll call her to the phone.» Well! Maybe I had better not forget about her.

When Elizabeth got back from Chautauqua someone told her I had tried to contact her a week previously but had left for Canada and was going to Columbia. Elizabeth went down to Columbia to say goodbye to an aunt and thought she might contact me there. She returned to New York feeling somewhat the same way I felt about the whole frustrating business! And suddenly my call to Kennedy House, and there she was on the phone, sounding a little flustered, trying to make arrangements to see me for a date. It was Friday evening and my bus left for Columbia on Sunday night. Her plane was leaving a day or two later. We had two days together to talk and see what we felt God had in store for us.

«How about it?» I asked her a few minutes after we met, «Can I ask you the same question I asked on our first walk together at Elat? Will you marry me?»

«I can't,» she said. «My mission has given me an extra year of furlough in order to get special training at Peabody Teachers Training College in Nashville; they expect me to teach in the children's school which starts in a week or so. I cannot break my word to the mission.»

«Well, how about a year from now?»

«Impossible.»

«Two years, then?»

«I can't promise, but who knows what may happen in two years. Maybe I'll be more free to say yes then.»

«O.K.,» I told her, «I will wait for two years. It will give us plenty of time to consider whether we are in love or not. In the meantime, if you fall in love with someone else, feel free to marry him and I'll do the same.» And on these terms we parted and said goodbye.

I was somewhat apprehensive about going back to college. I was twenty-nine years old and the thought of sitting in classes with teenagers made me squirm. But I was pleasantly surprised to discover that more than fifty per cent of the fellows in the entering class were in their late twenties and thirties and some in their forties. Many of them were G.I.'s taking advantage of the G.I. educational bill. My roommate had fought in the Pacific with the Marines and it was while out there fighting as a soldier he received his missionary call! We had great fellowship from the moment we met until we graduated and we still keep in touch. Bill has served many years in Africa with the Sudan Interior Mission.

Life as a student at Columbia Bible College was a constant challenge to me. I didn't find the courses difficult, except for one or two. I told Miss Warren, the registrar, that I would like to graduate, if possible, at the end of two years. She smiled at me, politely, and told me I would receive a year's credit for my work in Britain, and if I was willing to carry a heavy load and do summer school, then perhaps I might make it. I was willing.

I took 22 hours of classes the first semester and 25 years the second semester and did summer school. I was constantly in classes. I never knew what year I was in because Miss Warren fixed my schedule, so that I was taking freshman, sophomore, junior and senior classes when there was no conflict with any of these. It was rugged. I was permitted to live in the graduate dormitory, which meant I could study late at night when the curfew bell rang in the undergraduate dorms. One or two of the professors had the habit of speaking slowly in class, so I learned to follow their lectures, take notes, and at the same time prepare other assignments. This helped tremendously.

Because of my heavy schedule I was under constant pressure, and hated to take time off for sports or leisure. I only dated twice in two years. Occasionally I wrote a letter to Betty.

At the end of eight months I had spent all the money I had when I first arrived in the States. Suddenly it was gone. I had spent more money getting to Columbia than I had anticipated. Now I began to pray in earnest that God would supply my needs through preaching, which seemed to be the easiest way to find money. I could not preach often, however, as many weekends I was called to go out on student teams, which really taxed my study time and left little time for work. It was a college principle that all monies received by student teams go to the support of the Christian service program. So I had to trust the Lord to enable me to keep up with my studies, do my Christian service assignments and try to find a few hours to work in order to pay my fees.

After summer school in 1947 I really felt exhausted. I felt I couldn't keep up the kind of program I had been doing for very long. Besides, I knew I could not graduate at the end of two years, because no matter how hard I worked I would still lack eight hours of credits in order to graduate.

I went to work at Ben Lippen conference in Ashville, N.C., to try to earn more money for the next year's school expenses. It was hard to earn any money because we were obliged to work four hours a day for room and board. For an eight-hour day we could only earn three dollars. And dish-washing was hot, thirsty work, especially when the dish-washing machine broke down and we had to wash dishes by hand!

One morning Dr. McQuilkin came into the kitchen and said to me, «Bob, the speaker for the young people's meetings can't come for three days; come and share some of your experiences in Africa with the young people.» I did that, and at the end of the week I was given an honorarium which was more than I could earn in two weeks washing dishes!

That summer I really felt discouraged because I knew if I could not get those missing credits it would upset all my plans for entering a seminary in the fall of 1948. I could not understand why the College had given me so few credits for all the studies I had done in Europe at the Bible College of Wales, the Missionary School of Medicine and the Alliance Francaise. I felt low.

To add to my discouragement and confusion and my doubts about staying on at Columbia—I had begun to think of going to some college where I might get more credits—a well-meaning friend came to me at the conference and offered to pay all my expenses if I were to go to a certain denominational college and seminary. When I expressed my doubts about their theological position, especially in the seminary, he said to me, «Bob, some of those professors would give their right arm to have your simple faith in God!» I wasn't convinced with his argument but I must confess it was a great temptation and I almost accepted his offer. Instead of doing this, however, I went to talk with Dr. McQuilkin and share with him my frustrations about not being able to graduate at the end of 1948 school year.

I had learned that CBC was going to add French courses, Hebrew and nursing courses to the curriculum the following year. So I felt I had some grounds for asking for more credits as I had done work in all three fields. Fortunately the Dean of the faculty was at Ben Lippen that weekend and he and Dr. McQuilkin discussed my case. The happy result was that I was given another 18 credits, which made my second year at CBC easier and I was able to find work that I could do with ease to pay off my debts. The pressure was off and I graduated cum laude. Praise the Lord!

I learned so much about walking with the Lord at Columbia Bible College. I can never praise God enough for having led me there. I have had the privilege of working with godly men in three different continents and on different mission fields, but when I look back over these forty years I know of no man who had a greater spiritual influence in my life than Dr. Robert McQuilkin. I loved him from the moment I met him, not because, as he smilingly told me once, he and I were two Irish Bobs - his family came from Northern Ireland - but I loved him because he lived what he preached. He taught and preached the victorious Christian life and he lived it to the full. I recall that a roommate I had in my second year was really annoyed with something Dr. McQuilkin had said that had convicted him. When he was telling me of the incident he said, «Oh, McQuilkin, he could preach the victorious life from every verse in the first ten chapters of I Chronicles!»

Not only was I blessed and challenged by the victorious life message emphasized by Dr. McQuilkin, but also by the tremendous missionary vision of the President, which was shared by faculty, staff and students. As a missionary recently returned from Africa I was thrilled to be a part of the Foreign Missions Fellowship at CBC. I was amazed at the enthusiasm of the prayer-group leaders and their knowledge of the countries their prayer group represented.

I had the privilege of attending and speaking at the first Toccoa Falls missionary conference that was sponsored by the FMF groups of Columbia Bible College and Toccoa Falls Bible College. There were just two other missionary speakers and myself and about a hundred students from the two Bible colleges. That conference in 1947 was to be the forerunner of many that would follow, attended by hundreds of students, with many missions anxious to be represented.

It was at CBC that I had the vision of starting a similar work in Europe at the European Bible Institute called the European Students Missionary Association (ESMA), which now has chapters in eighteen Bible Institutes and Colleges. At its recent MISSION-80, organized and directed by an EBI graduate, Eric Gay, it attracted 7,000 students and 200 missionaries, representing scores of missions throughout the world. When MISSION-76 was organized in Lausanne, Switzerland, 3,000 students attended. Four years later it was more than doubled in number. If a similar MISSION is held in four more years, it may be as big as the same type of conference held in Urbana, USA. A more detailed report of this conference will be given in Eric Gay's testimony in the chapter «Training Timothys.»

In my last semester at CBC the Lord provided me with a job by which I could earn enough money to pay all my college expenses and also buy a wedding set! Oh, yes, I did send an ultimatum to Elizabeth, mostly as a joke. I wrote to her in one of my letters a few months before my graduation, «If you don't come home by June, I may marry one of these southern girls.» I received a cable from her saying, «Coming home June Betty.» A letter quickly followed saying that she was getting replaced at the children's school and expected to be in New York on June 3rd and we could get married on June 19.

My work was very pleasant. Dr. Harry Clark, a professor at the University of South Carolina, had been stricken with a stroke. Both he and his wife wanted a male nurse and had called the college to see if there were one among the students. Mr. Munro, the dean of men, remembered I had had some medical training and offered me the job. It was not complicated and consisted mostly of taking care of his essential needs. Dr. and Mrs. Clark were both fine Christians and were delighted to have a Bible college fellow as his nurse.

Dr. Clark paid me well. He taught religious studies. He was too ill to read and mark the assignments that were sent in by students doing his courses by correspondence. I was able to read these for him and mark them as well. I earned enough money from the Clarks to pay all our wedding expenses. Not too long after our wedding I learned that he had died. Betty and I were married in a small Presbyterian church in Cincinnati, Ohio, where her sister was a member.

After our wedding we headed for Winona Lake where I had been accepted as a student in Grace Theological Seminary. I only learned a short time before our wedding that my wife had been raised and educated in this small community. Among our wedding gifts was an unusual one. One of Betty's closest friends in Winona Lake offered us an upstairs apartment in her house, overlooking the lake, rent free, for three months, as a wedding present. It was beautiful. I was also ignorant of the fact that Winona Lake has a summer-long missionary and Bible conference, where well-known Bible teachers and preachers, from all over the world, come to minister each summer. What an ideal place for a honeymoon!

Our honeymoon was rudely interrupted, however, by a letter from the Immigration Department in Philadelphia, informing me that my student visa had expired, as I was no longer studying in a government-approved institution. I was given seventy-two hours to leave the country.

I went immediately to see Dr. Hoyt, Dean of the faculty at Grace Seminary, to ask him for an explanation. When I had applied to the seminary four months previously I had asked Dr. Hoyt if Grace Seminary was an approved school to accept foreign students. I was the first one to apply to the school. Dr. Hoyt had written to me to say that this was a mere formality and everything would be in order for me to enter in the fall. But the approval had not yet come, in spite of the fact that he had written to Washington several times. He showed me the file of correspondence with no positive answer from the government. He was distressed about the whole situation and urged me to go, personally, to Philadelphia and take his file with me. «Don't worry over it,» he said. «I'm sure everything will be all right.»

Don't worry about it! This was easier said than done. I was already in the country illegally as it had taken the letter two weeks to reach me. We immediately packed our suitcases and took a bus to Philadelphia. When we entered the Immigration Office and stated our business, we were sent from one office to another. No one seemed to know how to advise us on why the school had not been registered or how to go about doing this. Finally, one of them said to me, «Why don't you go down to Washington and try there?»

By this time I not only felt exasperated by their bureaucratic attitude, but was a little angry at their indifference and total lack of sympathy for our situation. I was just another immigration statistic! I told them we had no intention of going anywhere until we spoke with the director of the department. One of the men called a secretary and told her to take us to the director's office.

The director received us kindly and told us he was sorry we had come all the way to Philadelphia, but neither the Philadelphia nor the Washington immigration offices had any jurisdiction over foreigners living in northern Indiana; I should have gone to the immigration office in Chicago. How were we to know? There was nothing to do but go back home and then up to Chicago. We thanked him and got the bus back to Winona Lake. I was almost three weeks, now, illegally in the country and expected a policeman to arrive any day on our doorstep to arrest me.

In Chicago they told us we would have to go to Toledo, Ohio. I didn't believe it, after our experience in Philadelphia, and insisted that they check the records again. They did and rather shamefacedly they admitted that Winona Lake was not in the Ohio jurisdiction, but we had to go to South Bend, Indiana. Well, at least, South Bend was on our way home, so we went directly to the immigration office there, and for the first time met someone who seemed to know what he was talking about. We explained the whole situation to him and he said to us, «First of all, let me ask you a few questions about yourselves, so I can better understand your problem and see how I can help you.» We were encouraged. He addressed himself to me first and then to Betty.

«Where were you born, when did you come to this country and how long do you wish to stay?» I answered all his questions.

«One final question, is your wife an American citizen?»

«Oh, yes,» I told him. «She was born of American parents.»

Turning to Betty, he asked her, «Where were you born?»

«In Cameroon, West Africa,» she answered.

«Do you have a birth certificate?» was his next question.

«No, I don't, but I do have an affidavit of birth, signed by the Presbyterian missionary doctor who was present at my birth, as well as one from his wife.»

«O.K. Were both of your parents Americans, and if so where were they born?»

«Yes, my father was born in Flat Rock, Illinois, and my mother in Tipton, Iowa.»

«Were they legally married?»

«Oh yes, of course.»

«Do you have their marriage certificate as proof of this? Do you know where they were married?»

I heard Betty softly groan, «Oh, dear.» «No sir, I don't have their marriage certificate; I believe one of my sisters in Tennessee has it. My parents were married on a German ship going to Africa and the ship was later sunk, but I am sure the captain who married them also gave them a legal marriage certificate, because I have seen it.»

The official looked at us and said slowly, «Listen, young people, you will have to find that marriage certificate or there is not much I can do to help you. Once you have found it and can prove your own citizenship, then come back to me and I'll tell you how to help your husband, if he should ever wish to become an American citizen.»

«You cannot do this,» he said, looking at me, «until you leave this country and reapply to return. To do this and get an entry visa you must leave the country. You can go to Mexico, or Canada or Ireland. I would suggest you go to Canada, as it is the nearest.»

We both said in one voice. «Canada! We have friends there.»

«O.K., if you do find your parents' marriage certificate, you really don't need to come back here; I'll tell you right now what you must do. When you enter Canada, do not tell the Canadian authorities the purpose of your visit. If you have friends, you are going to see your friends. Of course, if they ask you directly the real purpose of your visit, you will have to tell them the truth. But here is the problem. One is not permitted by the Canadian authorities to enter Canada as a visitor in order to apply for a permanent U.S. visa. But you have no choice so you will have to take a chance on it. Once you are in Canada, simply go to the nearest American consulate and apply for a permanent visa like millions of Irishmen before you. If you have 'the luck of the Irish' you'll get one.» He grinned and we smiled although we felt more like crying!

Back once again in Winona Lake. It was the second week in August. Classes began the first week of September. A friend loaned us a car and we made a fast trip to Ashville, N.C. to see if Betty's oldest sister had the marriage certificate. Arta Grace had boxes of letters from her parents, written to various members of the family. Some were written a few days before the wedding, some a few days after, but none about the wedding itself and no marriage certificate. Arta Grace thought it was lost although she had remembered seeing it in one of the other sisters' homes.

We left Ashville wondering what we were going to do if we didn't find this certificate. We stopped off in Cincinnati to see Betty's sister, Esther. She was surprised to see us and said, «What is the reason for this unexpected visit?» We told her. «Why, I have the certificate upstairs in my bedroom drawer.» Hallelujah! Our search was over. We got home, returned the car, and once again packed our suitcases for another bus journey.

We arrived in Detroit and took a local bus over to Windsor, Canada. I told Betty to let me do the talking. While I was getting our suitcases off the bus, my wife had gone ahead and was standing at the immigration office looking slightly embarrassed. The immigration officer had asked her why she was going into Canada and she simply said to him, «Ask my husband, when he comes.»

The officer looked at our suitcases and looked at me, and then asked me the question I was really expecting, «What is the purpose of your visit to Canada?»

«Well, sir,» I told him. «I'll be honest with you. We have come to Canada in order to apply for an American visa.»

«Sorry,» he said. «I can't let you in.»

I laughed when he said this. «What's so funny?» he asked me.

«Nothing's funny,» I replied. «I just laughed because we can't—at least *I* can't go back into the United States. My student visa has expired and they wouldn't let me in if I went back. What are you going to do about it? We are already on Canadian soil.»

He was perplexed and didn't know what to do, except call his superior, who listened patiently and sympathetically to our story.

«Well,» he said, «I will give you a fourteen-day visa to see if you can obtain a U.S. visa, but if you don't succeed, you will have to return to Ireland.»

«Thank you, we'll be happy to accept your fourteen days of grace!» We couldn't do otherwise. We had about $200 and I wondered how far it would go. I knew it wouldn't pay for our tickets to Ireland. The Lord was going to have to undertake for us and answer the many prayers we had offered up to Him the past few weeks.

As soon as we found a room, we went straight to the American consulate. I was told I would need a medical certificate, a chest X-ray, and a police certificate to say I had committed no crimes. I had to get this certificate from police in every country I had lived in since I was fifteen years old. I was flabbergasted. I told the consul it would be well nigh impossible for me to get such a certificate as I had lived in Ireland, France, Liberia and Spanish Guinea, and besides I only had a fourteen-day visa.

«Well, young fellow, I'll tell you what to do,» he said to me. «Here is the name and address of the chief of police in Windsor; go and see him and explain to him your difficulty; he has kept a lot of young men like you out of prison.»

«Are you kidding me?» I asked him.

«No, no, I'm not kidding you; I mean it. I know he will do what he can to help you.»

That same afternoon we made an appointment to see the chief of police at eight o'clock in his home. He was a very nice person, indeed. In fact, we later discovered that he was a Christian and an elder in the Presbyterian church, and knew of Betty's parents and their work in Cameroon.

While his wife was making tea for us, he talked, in fact did most of the talking, and from time to time would ask us a simple question. This went on for about an hour, and suddenly we both realized that, in a very diplomatic way, he had heard our life story! Then he asked my wife what her maiden name was. When she told him, he said, «Why I know your parents, although I have never met them. But I have been reading about their work in Cameroon for a long time. I am interested in the Presbyterian Mission in Africa. So you were Miss Elizabeth Christine Hope? Well, it is nice to meet at least one Hope daughter in person.» By this time he had no doubts about our integrity and the real purpose of our wanting an American visa.

Then we got down to the practical business of how to obtain those police certificates. «All of them will be easy to get except the one from Spanish Guinea; that may be hard. I can send cables and get back an answer in a few days, a week at most. But it will cost you about $75 for the cables,» he told me.

I explained to him the situation in Spanish Guinea as I had known it. «They might even give me a bad record if the wrong kind of police chief is in office who hates evangelical work,» and I told him of some of my personal experiences with these ungodly officials.

«Well, we'll worry about that if and when it happens, and besides it would be written in Spanish and my Spanish is not too good! So don't worry about it.»

We knew that everything was going to be all right. It was the first time in a month that we really felt encouraged. Sure enough, a week later we got a call from the police telling us all the replies had come back. «And do you know what?» the chief of police said. «The one from Spanish Guinea is written in English and gives you a good report.» It was unbelieveable. Two years later I learned what had happened in Spanish Guinea when the cable arrived from the Windsor police.

Mac and Lois McNeill came to visit us in Winona Lake, and the first thing he said after greeting us was, «Hey, what were you doing in Windsor a couple of years ago? Were you in some kind of trouble with the police?»

«No, I wasn't in any trouble with the police,» I told him. «But I did have a problem with the American consul, who wouldn't furnish me a visa until I had gotten a police certificate from every country I had lived in, including Spanish Guinea. But what do you know about this?»

«Why, I know everything about it,» he grinned. «I happened to drop into the police station in Bata to greet the chief of police and I found him holding a cable in his hand and shaking his head.

»'Ah, Señor McNeill,' he said, 'I am so glad you have come in. I need your help. Do you know a certain Don Roberto Munn, who was supposed to have lived here between 1942 and 1945?' He showed me the cable and I translated it for him. Then he asked me to write the answer for him!»

So it was Mac who wrote the cable and gave me a good report. It is amazing to see how God uses seemingly inconsequential circumstances, like a polite visit by a missionary to a chief of police in order to maintain good public relations and the casual visit was part of God's wonderful plan to meet the need of another missionary thousands of miles away. I repeat, «As for God his way is perfect,» and «All things work together for good to them that love God...»

The next morning we went to the consulate rejoicing in the wonderful way God had undertaken for us, enabling us to get all the required documents and leaving us enough money to get home to Winona Lake. When we handed the consul the police certificates and the other documents, he examined them carefully. Then he put them all in a large envelope and told us to come back at the end of October and we would receive our visa.

«The end of October?» I almost gasped out the words. «Sir, I am supposed to register for school next Tuesday and today is Friday.»

«Oh, you are? But didn't you know that you applied for a quota visa, and not a student visa?» he asked me.

«No, sir, I didn't know.» And I confessed my ignorance of the immigration laws of the United States. «But if you can permit me to enter today, I sure would appreciate it.»

He had placed my envelope at the bottom of a pile of others, undoubtedly those who were ahead of me. He slowly took it out again and handed it to me. «Give this envelope to the immigration office on the other side» was all he said to me.

When we finally got over to Detroit one day before our fourteen-day visa expired, as we walked up to the immigration officer, furnished with our entry visa, we felt good. When the officer opened it and read all the documents, he said to us, «You are not supposed to enter the United States until the end of October, but now you are here and I have broken the seal on this envelope. I guess it won't make much difference. Good luck to you.»

Well, we knew that it had been more than good luck that had enabled us to enter the U.S.A. It was the Lord, who had promised, «Behold I set before you an open door and no man can shut it.» Praise God!

We had four days to recover from our mental and physical tiredness and prepare ourselves for the intensive course of study at Grace Theological Seminary. This was to be the second stage of our preparation in the west.

CHAPTER 8

A Macedonian Call

> And a vision appeared unto Paul in the night; there stood a man of Macedonia, and prayed him, saying, Come over into Macedonia and help us.
>
> And after he had seen the vision, immediately we endeavoured to go into Macedonia, assuredly gathering that the Lord had called us for to preach the gospel unto them.
>
> (Acts 16:9-10)

Life at Grace Theological Seminary as a married student was so different from life as a single student at Columbia Bible College. For one thing, the courses were more difficult, the assignments longer and the off-campus atmosphere a contrast to dormitory life at college. One thing I did discover fast was that it was not cheaper for two to live than one. When Sandra Jo and Jim were born, it cost even more for four! But God's promise and provision never changes nor fails. What we had proved as a single student was just as true as a married student.

There was one big difference: Winona Lake was not heavily industrialized and jobs were not for the asking. I was fortunate to find a humble job of cleaning the Winona Conference offices and for three years I worked on the conference grounds. In the summer I doubled up as a policeman and later as deputy sheriff of Kosciusko County.

During the three years at Winona Lake I did every kind of work imaginable to support our family, but the job I preferred and which paid me most was teaching Franch. How often down through the years I had wondered why I had worked and sweated so hard to get that French teaching diploma at the Alliance Francaise in Paris. It was in Winona Lake that I came to understand why. First of all, it was the major means of providing for my family and secondly, and most important, God used it to turn our eyes towards France as a mission field.

The money I was earning those first weeks in Winona Lake was just barely enough to put food on the table. At the end of September we would have to start paying rent for our apartment, as our three months rent-free wedding present was about to expire. I had prayed at CBC that God would provide me with a job that would pay well and yet leave me time for my studies. I prayed the same prayer at Grace Seminary, and the Lord answered this prayer in a very interesting manner.

One evening a married student and his wife came to our apartment and Charlie said to me, «Bob, someone told me you understand French and might be willing to help me and my wife with our French studies.» They were prospective candidates for missionary work in French-speaking Africa. I told them that I would be glad to help them.

«Well,» he said, «if you do, we won't ask you to do it for nothing. We'll be glad to pay you a dollar an hour.» I was earning eighty cents an hour cleaning the offices. I agreed and after they left, I said to Betty, «It would be good if we could find another couple or several who need help!» Well, what do you know, our friends came the next evening for their lessons and brought another couple with them, so I was paid two dollars an hour. This continued for several lessons and it took very little preparation for me as they knew so little of the language that anything I taught them was progress.

Unknown to me these students spoke with the registrar of the college and told him they were getting help from one of the seminary students with their French. «In fact,» they added, «this fellow knows more French than our teacher, and is better qualified to teach. She has told us that she doesn't care to teach in college as her husband is ill and she would like to be able to break her contract. Why don't you ask Bob Munn to teach her class? We think he would be happy to do it.» The registrar learned that it was true what the students had told him, that she did want to be released, and so that is how I was asked to teach French, which I was happy to do.

When I went for an interview and the registrar learned that I had a French diploma from the *Alliance Francaise,* he offered me the job and told me they would pay me five dollars a teaching hour plus the same amount for each examination hour. I could hardly believe my ears. I quickly accepted the offer and ran home to tell Betty, «I have a teaching job and you'll never believe what they are going to pay me, five dollars an hour.» That was a lot of money in 1948. It was such a wonderful answer to prayer for us that we felt God had some other purpose in our finding this particular job than simply providing for our financial needs.

I had eight students in my class, all of them accepted candidates for missionary work in the Central African Republic. It was a joy to teach them and they never complained no matter how heavy the assignments I gave them. They were all anxious to learn as much of the language as they could before going over to France. They were more than average students and made good grades.

As soon as they had grasped the basics of French grammar I gave them assignments not usually taught in college French courses. I wrote to Nogent Bible Institute, where I had studied French for a while, and purchased French Bibles and hymnbooks. The hymnbook contained many of the well known English hymns that had been translated by Dr. Ruben Saillens, so the tunes were familiar. My students had to memorize some of these hymns, learn to read the French Bible and translate passages from the gospels into English.

By the end of the year they were all confident that they could go to France and make themselves understood and carry on a simple conversation. They enrolled at the *Alliance Francaise* and some of them received the diploma. This was a great encouragement to me as a teacher and also an encouragement to their mission, which actually paid my salary.

So for the next two years I had a similar class of prospective missionary candidates and it was a great satisfaction to have a part in their preparation for missionary work in Africa. Besides, those three years of teaching on the faculty of Grace College gave me the assurance that I could communicate acceptably well with students. I was glad in more ways than one that God led me to Grace Theological Seminary. He did a new thing for me.

The three years at Grace passed very quickly. As the last semester of my third year approached, I said to Betty one afternoon, after I had spent a couple of hours marking French papers for my class, «You know, sometimes I wonder why the Lord provided me with this particular teaching job, apart from its having met our financial needs these past three years. You remember how the Lord promised His people, 'I will make a way for you in the wilderness?' I wonder what sort of way the Lord is going to make for us.»

We had been approached by the Director of a denominational mission to work for them in Africa. I had been associated with the WEC for nearly ten years and I felt that God was going to lead us again into a non-denominational work. In three months I would receive my diploma. I had been studying for five years without a break. I was anxious to get back again into foreign missionary service.

«Maybe the Lord is going to lead us to a French-speaking field,» Betty said, «and that is why He has given you this opportunity to teach French for the past three years.»

«Look, Cameroon is out, I said to her. «We have been out of touch with the WEC for years; we could apply to WEC but I don't feel that this is God's will. I think He has something entirely new for us. I read a promise the other day in Isaiah 43:19, «Behold I will do a new thing: now it shall spring forth, shall ye not know it? I will even make a way in the wilderness and rivers in the desert....» What do you think it means?»

«Perhaps it means that God is going to lead us to France,» Betty replied.

«I don't see how He will. I don't know any missions working in France and besides I want to teach in a Bible school. 'I will make a way in the wilderness, and rivers in the desert....' Well, maybe it does mean that God is going to make the way clear for us, soon. Maybe He *will* lead us to France.»

I thought about this possibility off and on for the next several weeks. Then one afternoon in a student missionary prayer meeting, one of the fellows handed me a newsletter from the European Bible Institute and said, «Bob, here is something that might interest you; it is about France.» I took the letter and glanced at it. Across the top of the letter was the name of the organization. It read, EUROPEAN BIBLE INSTITUTE - INSTITUT BIBLIQUE EUROPEEN and a Chicago address.

The letter was written by Noel O. Lyons, North American representative of the European Bible Institute and he began his letter thus, «This is a Macedonia call; come over into France and help us.»

You talk about being challenged by a statement. Here it was, the challenge I had been subconsciously waiting for. *«Come over into France and help us.»* Right there, after I finished reading the letter, I bowed my head and prayed, «Lord, if this call is from You to me, personally, I'll go. Here am I, send me.»

That evening after Betty had put the children to bed, I said to her, «Honey, the Lord has answered our prayers for guidance about our future missionary service. I believe He is going to lead me to teach in a French Bible Institute. Listen to this letter.» I read it to her, and this is what it said, «The European Bible Institute desperately needs teachers with a good knowledge of French and who preferably have had some missionary and teaching experience. Come over and help us; we need you right now.»

«What do you think Betty?» I asked her. «Is this God's call to us?»

166

«Well, Bob, if you feel that God is calling you to teach in this school, I am willing to go. But let us pray some more about it for a few weeks, at least, to see if we feel differently about it, and if we don't, then let us go ahead and apply to this school and go over and help them. It does seem like it is the very place that God has prepared for you and it is the kind of opportunity you have been praying for.»

I wrote to the organization and told them of our interest and willingness to join them, and something of our background and experience, but I didn't hear from them. Several weeks passed and I began to wonder if the need was as great as they had said it was. Also I wondered if such a school as the European Bible Institute existed, because most people whom I thought might know about it professed their ignorance of the existence of such an organization.

One evening I was cleaning the conference offices and the conference secretary suddenly said to me, «Bob, what are you going to do when you finish your studies six weeks from now?»

I told her about the letter from the European Bible Institute, my response to it and the fact that we had not heard from them, and I mentioned Noel Lyon's name.

«There must be a mistake somewhere,» Louise told me. «I know this man and he is not the kind of person to neglect answering this kind of letter. Maybe your letter didn't reach him. Let me see if he is still in his office, because he often works late.»

She picked up the phone, and, sure enough, Mr. Lyons was there and he talked to me immediately. For some reason he had not received my letter of enquiry. He told me he was flying to France the very next day and would give me a positive answer, he thought, when he returned in ten days time.

Mr. Lyons was as good as his word. Immediately after he returned he wrote me a long letter sharing with me the hopes and aspirations of the three missionaries, Dr. and Mrs. Robert Evans and Irene Bonjour. They were trying to lay the groundwork for the Bible school. An old building had been purchased in the suburbs of Paris. An evening school had begun three months before. They hoped we could find support quickly, in order to join them for the second semester of the evening school in September. Mr. Lyons arranged for Betty and me to meet the Board of the European Bible Institute after my graduation in May.

In my last year at Grace Seminary I had been elected student body president and was asked to give the valedictory address in the new chapel of the brand new campus that Grace was building. For years the seminary had rented rooms on the top floor of the Free Methodist Publishing House in Winona Lake. The seminary had purchased land and the first building, the McClain Memorial Chapel would be completed in time for the graduation services.

One day I met Dr. McClain, President of Grace Seminary and College, and he joked with me about the fact that I was going to beat him to it.

«Beat you to what, sir?» I asked him.

«Why, to preaching the first sermon in the new chapel,» he answered. «The baccalaureate sermon will be the first and you will be preaching it!»

I was as much amused as he was. I shall always praise God for the sound Biblical and doctrinal teaching I received from this man of God. I have taught his doctrine courses in France, Guatemala, Belgium and the Republic of Ireland.

A few days later the editor of the year book asked me what I was going to do after graduation, as he wished to write something for the year book. «Well, if you had come several days earlier I wouldn't have known, but now I know. I am going to teach in a Bible school in France. It is called the European Bible Institute.»

«Have you already been accepted by the Board of the Mission?» he asked me.

«Well, not yet, but we will be seeing the Board next month and fully expect to be accepted,» I told him.

The following week Betty and I did go to Chicago to the small office, a three room affair, where the European Bible Institute, later to become known as the Greater Europe Mission, had its headquarters. When we entered, Mr. Lyons introduced us to five businessmen who comprised the Board. After formal greetings, Mr. Lyons told them how he had contacted us and then asked each of us to give our testimony, which took a few minutes. When we had finished, one of the men turned to the others and said, «I think they are a pretty nice couple and we ought to invite them to join the faculty of the European Bible Institute.»

They all agreed, and that was how we joined the EBI faculty. All so simple and never to be repeated by later candidates, because the school grew into a large mission. Anyone applying to the Greater Europe Mission today might find it hard to believe what we have just written. But I have told it like it was.

As soon as my graduation was over I joined Mr. Lyons in Chicago and spent Monday through Friday every week, for three months, contacting people and trying to interest them in the work of EBI. Every morning Mr. Lyons would give me several scores of names and addresses of people in Chicago and the greater Chicago area. I would try to visit as many of these as possible and talk to them about the need of France. I really didn't have much to talk about.

We had one old building in the process of being renovated. Evening school had just started and met in rented rooms in Paris. The day school had not yet begun. We had as yet no students and only a few prospective students in sight.

Bob Evans had been European Director of Youth for Christ and had felt led of the Lord to establish the European Bible Institute as a more effective way of evangelizing Europeans. I agreed 100 % with his vision, but so far, it was mostly vision and not too substantial at that. Bob and his wife Jeanette, and Irene were trying to make the old building in Chatou habitable, hoping to open it as a day school in January 1952. The story of this old building and its eventual transformation into a Bible institute has been told in more detail in *TROPHIES OF GRACE - The Story of Men and Women of God at the European Bible Institute,* published by the Greater Europe Mission.

I must confess I did not enjoy this visitation work at all. Most of the people received me kindly, but some told me rather rudely they were not interested in France or any other foreign place; USA needed missionaries at home, and not to call again.

It wasn't easy and I was seeing very little visible results from my personal visitation. But in looking back over what seemed a fruitless and unsuccessful summer, there were at least two bright spots in the whole picture.

One day I went out to the Wheaton area to talk with some friends of Bob and Jeanette Evans. Mr. Lyons had given me their address. It was a hot day and I was thirsty. When I rang the bell, Matthew Evans, no relation of Robert Evans, invited me in, and introduced me to his wife Stevania.

«Before you say anything,» he told me, «you look

170

thirsty; let me get you a coke.» Then he asked me the reason for my visit and I told him.

«We are glad you came,» he said. «My wife and I are interested in Europe and we will help you.» And they did. They took on some of our support and continued to send it faithfully for many years. When Mr. Evans died, his wife sent a memorial gift to EBI to purchase books for the EBI library. Stevania is in a retirement home but continues to pray for us and support us. We thank the Lord for every remembrance of Matthew and Stevania Evans, faithful prayer-helpers.

The second bright spot was the meeting of an older couple in north Chicago. I was warmly welcomed into their home, really a rare experience during that summer. When I shared with them our missionary hopes, Mr. Crippen turned to his wife and said, «Dear, I believe we can pay the Munns' passage to France,» and in so saying, he wrote me a check for $1200. He went to be with Christ a few months later. I never asked him for this money—I have never asked anyone for money—but his spontaneous gift warmed and encouraged my heart.

September 1951 came and the Evans were anxious for us to get over to France for the second term of the Evening School, which started the first week in October. They also hoped to have the building in Chatou ready for students to enter in January 1952. We prayed earnestly that God would meet our needs and make it possible for us to join them on time. Mr. Lyons figured we would need $250 a month for our living expenses. Two of our seminary friends had promised to support us, $125 a month. Another small church in Palestine, Indiana promised $25 a month. This was all we had promised by the second week in September. I told Mr. Lyons we would go to France and trust the Lord to supply our needs there. He had done it before and I believed He would do it again; and besides, we had our passage money.

«O.K.,» he said, «I will book a passage for you on the Queen Elizabeth for September 20 and we'll trust God to send in the needed $100.» We agreed to this.

Just one week before we were scheduled to leave Winona Lake for New York, we attended the last prayer meeting in our church in Mentone, Indiana. That evening one of the members called Betty and me to sit beside him and his wife.

«How is your support coming in?» he asked me.

«I still need $100 a month for full support,» I told him.

Turning to his wife he asked her, «How much were we going to pledge for the Munns?»

«$1,000 a year,» she said.

«Well, I don't see why we can't make it $1,200, do you?»

«No, that's O.K. with me. If they need $1,200, they need $1,200.»

That is how God answered our prayer for support, one week before we left for France.

We arrived in New York, sold our car to a friend and boarded the Queen Elizabeth. There was a letter for us in our cabin from Mr. Lyons, saying, «Bon voyage. I'm glad you answered the Macedonian call.» So were we. In spite of some wilderness experiences and «dry spots» that lay ahead, the Lord was faithful and did make a way for us in the wilderness and rivers in the desert. «Faithful is he that calleth you, who also will do it.»

I don't believe the apostle Paul looked forward with any greater interest to meeting the man of Macedonia, which turned out to be a woman, than we were to meet some of the «Lydias» and «Timothys»

172

whom God would bring across our path. We sailed across the Atlantic with deep peace and joy in our hearts as the result of obedience to God's call, and with an earnest expectation that He was going to do an entirely new thing for us. Some of the new things He did I have told in my book *TROPHIES OF GRACE.*

What we wanted with all our hearts to be able to say above all else was, «I was not disobedient to the heavenly vision.» By His grace we were not, and we have never regretted answering the call, «Come over into Macedonia and help us.»

But when divers were hardened and believed not, but spake evil of that way before the multitude, he departed from them, and separated the disciples, disputing daily in the school of one Tyrannus.

And this continued for the space of two years; so that all they that dwelt in Asia heard the word of the Lord Jesus, both Jews and Greeks.

CHAPTER 9

The European Bible Institute

But when divers were hardened and believed not, but spake evil of that way before the multitude, he departed from them, and separated the disciples, disputing daily in the school of one Tyrannus.

And this continued for the space of two years; so that all they that dwelt in Asia heard the word of the Lord Jesus, both Jews and Greeks.

(Acts 19:9-10)

There is always a tremendous challenge about the beginning of a new work, seeing faith become sight and a vision realized. I have often wondered what Paul and Silas thought as their ship left Troas «and came with a straight course to Samathracia, and the next day to Neapolis.» (Acts 16:11) There had been

175

no hesitation in their decision to obey the vision Paul had received from the Lord, because we read, «After he had seen the vision, *immediately* we endeavoured to go, assuredly gathering that the Lord had called us for to preach the gospel unto them.» (Acts 16:10)

There were, undoubtedly, plenty of uncertainties involved in this venture of faith, but there were also some strong unshakeable convictions demonstrated by these apostolic missionaries. They were convinced of their God-given vision; they knew the power of the gospel message they proclaimed; they were sure of God's call and the reason for which they were going to Macedonia - to preach the gospel. They expected to win souls for Christ.

But where was the man of Macedonia? Apparently, they never found him, unless Luke, the writer of the Acts, was he, as some Bible commentators believe. But in obedience to God's will they found Lydia, «whose heart the Lord opened so that she attended unto the things that were spoken of Paul.» (Acts 16:14) She and her household, probably a goodly number of people, believed and were baptized. They found the demon-possessed girl and by God's power exorcised the demon, possibly leading her to faith «in the most high God.» (Acts 16:17) They certainly found the jailor and his family, who believed and were baptized. (Acts 16:33)

It was not just one man of Macedonia who was won to Christ, although his salvation would have been worth the trip from Troas, but a company of people who found the Saviour, because of the obedience of Paul and Silas. And those believers met together to form the nucleus of the Philippian church, a church dear to the heart of the apostle Paul. He could say of the Philippians, every time he thought of them, he thanked God for them. When he prayed for them, it was with joy. (Philippians 1:3,5) It was this church at Philippi that he longed to see and have fellowship with. (Philippians 1:7,8) Born out of persecution and suffering, the Philippian church was one of Paul's greatest encouragements.

We also did a lot of wondering as we crossed the Atlantic on board the Queen Elizabeth en route to France, our «Macedonia». We felt somewhat in the same situation as Joshua when God told him, «...that you might know the way you must go, for you have not passed this way heretofore.» (Joshua 3:4) This was certainly a new way for us, but we were confident that the Lord had called us and we were demonstrating our obedience to His call. We knew He was going before us and that was all that mattered.

We had met Bob Evans briefly at a Youth for Christ conference in Winona Lake a few months before. He very kindly drove to Le Havre to meet us. Bob never looked better to us in all his life than he did that cool September morning standing on the quay to greet us and welcome us to France.

«Man, are we glad you made it! Praise the Lord! We have been praying that you would get here in time to teach at the Evening Bible School. We would like you to teach the Doctrine of the Person of Christ.»

«Whew,» I thought, «how can I do that?» True, I had been teaching French for three years at Grace College. It is one thing, however, to teach American students the rudiments of French grammar and a little French literature, but to teach a doctrine course to French students, two hours at a stretch, two evenings a week, was something else. «Suppose I don't understand their questions? Suppose I don't get my boxes through customs on time with my Bible notes?» These and a dozen other questions flashed through my mind.

«That you might know the way that you must go

for you have not passed this way heretofore.» But the Lord has passed this way, and He knows the way through the wilderness. If this is His way, He will help.

So I said to Bob, «O.K., brother, I'll be glad to teach the course. That is what we have come to France to do.»

Irene had booked a large room for us in a small family boarding-house, not far from where she and the Evans were living in Neuilly, a suburb of Paris. On the way to Paris, Bob stopped in the town of Chatou, about eight miles from the city, and said, «This is where the European Bible Institute will be located. Come and see the building the Lord has provided for us.»

We rang the bell and the caretaker, an elderly military looking man - he was an ex-gendarme - opened the large iron gates and let us into the property. The caretaker had not been paid by the former owner, so he had done no work on the building or gardens for several years. The small piece of land surrounding the house was covered with weeds two feet high. The 18-room building was solid, although devoid of all comfort. Inside, two men were working, installing plumbing and electricity and converting some of the larger rooms into smaller bedrooms for future students.

After going through the three-storey building, we returned to the ground floor and, before leaving the house, Bob Evans prayed a simple prayer of dedication, asking God to establish the European Bible Institute on a miracle basis. As we looked into the future with only three or four prospective students, with no ready cash on hand, and very few friends in Europe or the USA to stand behind us, financially, we knew that God would have to perform miracles if EBI was ever to become a reality.

But God did perform miracles and the old Chatou building was the home of the European Bible Institute for eight years, until it became too small to meet the growing needs of the student body. In 1960 the school moved twenty-five miles north of Paris to the beautiful seventy-room Chateau de Lamorlaye, surrounded by seventeen acres of delightful wooded park land. And EBI was to become the forerunner of nine other Bible institutes and a seminary, established by the Greater Europe Mission.

At this point in time over 400 students have been graduated from EBI and over 2,000 students from Greater Europe Mission schools throughout the continent.

But all of this was not accomplished without much hard work and dedication on the part of faculty, staff and students who came to EBI. Twenty-three of the twenty-five years we served in the Greater Europe Mission were spent as a Bible school teacher and administrator at the European Bible Institute. Along with others we saw the school grow into one of the largest missions in Europe, with Bible schools established in nine European countries, most of these modeled after EBI. To God be the glory; great things He has done.

About thirty young people faithfully attended the evening Bible School in Paris. For most of them it was not easy to do this. They worked in factories, offices, hospitals from 8 a.m. until 6 p.m. They didn't have time to return home for supper before the first class began, so brought sandwiches and coffee and ate their supper at the school. Four of these evening school students entered EBI when day classes began in Chatou on January 15, 1952. One other, a man in his forties, also wanted to enroll in the day school but was prevented by family responsibilities. When he retired at 65 years, he came out to Lamorlaye and enrolled as a student. George Laupretre graduated three years later, not only the oldest EBI grad ever, but one of its most faithful and loyal alumni. He told me on one occasion, «Mr. Munn, every day I went to my office and every day I returned home, I said to myself, 'One more day nearer to entering EBI!'»

After day classes began in Chatou it became increasingly difficult for the three faculty members—Bob Evans, Irene Bonjour and myself—to continue the evening school program, although we did it for nearly three more years. We had instituted a bi-lingual program of studies (French and English) in order to attract English-speaking Europeans to the Institute. English is the second language spoken in most European countries. It meant doubling our teaching load as we had to spend as much time preparing for two students as we did later for thirty or more in each section.

EBI began with nine students from four different countries and right from the beginning an international atmosphere was created that has characterized the Institute these many years. Students have enrolled from every western European country and the Near East. In fact, more than thirty nationalities have been represented among the student body with never less than a dozen at any given time. The truth of Galations 3:28 was demonstrated among the student body of EBI. «...for ye are all one in Christ Jesus.»

Only those who have had the opportunity of being «in on the ground floor» of EBI know something of the struggles we had to get EBI started. Our needs were legion. Almost all the students who came the first year had no money and jobs were scarce. There were enough repairs needing to be done on the property which provided work for students and was credited to their room and board. Classes were from 8 a.m. to 12:15 p.m., so the afternoons were free for work.

To find money to pay the utilities, repairs and food with none coming from students and very little from friends in Europe or the USA, certainly threw us upon the Lord as our only source of supply. Praise the Lord, He did supply our needs in many wonderful ways. God did establish EBI on a miracle basis, but we five missionaries also endeavored to answer our own prayers. We gave half of our salary to pay the basic needs of running the school.

That first year we took in missionary boarders who wished to learn French. We did not continue this policy the second year because our student body doubled the second semester, and for the next several years, it grew until we had fifty students enrolled. Some of these early struggles to get the Institute established is told in TROPHIES OF GRACE.

At the end of the first year the students were informed that the Institute could not provide enough work for all, and, in the future, everyone would be expected to pay his room and board. Tuition would be free. Some of those first year students felt perplexed. They came from poor families or from Catholic or Communist homes whose families were opposed to their being in a Bible school, or from small struggling churches who could not help them, financially. But they all came back and eight out of the nine finished the three-year course, which was a pretty high percentage to graduate from an entering class.

Many EBI graduates have testified that one of the most precious lessons they learned at EBI was to trust the Lord for their financial needs. As far as I can remember we never sent a student away from EBI for not being able to pay his board.

The first semester was in many ways a memorable one. The nine students whom God sent to us were precious young people. They came from France, Switzerland, Egyptian Sudan, and one Austrian girl who was born and raised in China made up the total. Eight of them, as we have already said, finished the three-year course and all except one are still in full-time Christian service.

I had fourteen hours of classes in the day school, four hours in the evening school, taught a two-hour Bible study every Friday evening in a town twenty miles from Chatou and preached almost every Sunday afternoon at EBI. It was a rough schedule and left very little time for anything except teaching and study. Irene and Bob also carried heavy loads. Often we wished we only taught in one language, which would have eased the academic pressure, at least. But if we had not decided to accept English-speaking students, many of the evangelical leaders in Europe today, who studied in the English section of EBI, would not have come to Chatou or Lamorlaye. See their testimonies in the 10th chapter.

Jeanette Evans acted as business manager and supervised the kitchen. Betty, with our two children aged 13 months and two years, had her hands full trying to learn the language, and do the Institute laundry. There was no possibility of studying the language for two years such as GEM missionaries enjoy today. Bob Evans was often away on speaking trips, recruiting students and doing public relations work for the Institute. Through his meetings and contacts many of the early students came to EBI, especially from Holland and Germany. All of us were constantly under pressure, but the Lord sustained us in every phase of the work. They were wonderful days and God taught us many lessons, lessons that could only have been learned in the context of a pioneer work.

The Lord kept His hand upon us physically those

first months. The kind of life we lived was hard on us as families. We ate with the students, who sometimes tried to tell us how to raise our children. Europeans are much more frank in some of these areas than we are. The children had several narrow escapes around the property which almost cost them their lives. Just one instance, and several just as dangerous could be mentioned. Our Jim, who was nearly three years old, and Sandra Jo, four, were visiting and playing with Bruce Evans, who was only two. The children were having a great time in Bruce's bedroom and Jeanette occasionally popped in to check on them. The French window of the bedroom was on a level with the outside gutter of the roof. The window was firmly closed and not easy for a child to open, but Sandra Jo must have opened it.

Suddenly Jeanette noticed that the children were unusually quiet and went to the bedroom to see what they were up to. To her horror she saw the window open and heard the children's voices out on the roof. The building had a sloping roof and the gutter which was about eighteen inches wide ran all the way around the building. When Jeanette put her head out of the window, she saw the three children standing about six feet away leaning precariously on the roof.

«Sandra Jo,» she said quietly, «just come back, honey, and don't stand up, just lean on the roof.»

All three children came back to the window in that way, and Jeanette grabbed each one and pulled him to safety. Then for about ten minutes she felt too weak to do anything. She came down to the ground floor and called me from a class to tell me the story of the children's escapade. It was my turn to feel weak! I dismissed my class as it was almost time for the bell to ring. I took Sandra Jo and Jim to our house and tried to tell them how dangerous it was to

183

do what they had done, and, to add weight to my words, I gave them both a little spanking.

After a few moments of crying, Sandra Jo dried her eyes and then, with a shrug of her shoulders, said to me, «You know, Daddy, it wasn't really very dangerous; it was just dangerous one time when Jim almost pushed Bruce off the roof!»

Miracle? Yes. «The angel of the Lord encampeth round about those who fear him and delivereth them.» (Psalm 34:7) I am quite convinced that the angel of the Lord, or their own guardian angel, was around our children that day on the roof. I didn't tell Jeanette for a long time what Sandra Jo had told me. Recently our daughter wrote to us and said, «Dad and Mom, I remember you told us that Jim and I had a childish game that we called 'Let's drive Dad and Mom crazy'. I laughed about it, but I don't laugh now when it seems that Vanessa and Arielle are playing the same game with Gerard and me.»

During the two years I studied at Columbia Bible College I was deeply impressed by two aspects of the college's philosophy of education. One was the principle of putting into practice what the student learned in the classroom. This principle was implemented very effectively by the whole student body, and very capably supervised by Mr. Tom Petty, Sr. Scores of people were brought to Christ in every walk of life through the Christian Service of Columbia Bible College students.

The other aspect of CBC which left a lasting impression upon me was the missionary vision and emphasis of the school. It seemed like more than fifty per cent of the student body was headed for foreign missionary work. I became deeply involved in both of these programs and vowed that, if I ever found myself teaching in a Bible College, I would push these programs as hard as I could.

184

At the European Bible Institute I had every opportunity to do exactly this. I was asked to supervise the Christian Service program of the Institute from its inception and I directed this program for twelve years. The missionary program came a few years later. Both of these have become a vital part of the EBI curriculum and both have resulted in hundreds of young people coming to know Christ as Saviour, and thousands of students, not only in GEM schools but in many others in Europe, have been challenged by the missionary vision of the European Students Missionary Association, which I had the privilege of initiating at the Institute in 1954. More about ESMA later.

For twelve years a bi-weekly meeting was held at EBI in English so that a number of English-speaking missionaries studying in Paris could have at least one service in English. They all felt they needed this spiritual fellowship with folk from other missions and EBI was a good neutral place for such. The meeting was very popular and also attracted American servicemen and their families from bases around the Paris area. This meeting also brought great blessing to the Institute and the generous offerings these good people gave supported the entire Christian Service program. Part of this program was door-to-door visitation and distribution of Scriptures and Christian literature, and much of the money given by missionaries and servicemen paid for this phase of our outreach.

Something completely new was added to the Christian Service program when students began to use gospel billposters, pasting them on walls, barn doors and anywhere the notice «Post No Bills» was absent. Billposting is a very important, as well as a very inexpensive, way of advertising in France. An English missionary couple, David Cole and his wife Pat, had been challenged by this means of advertising, simply because it was extensively and apparently successfully used by the French Communist Party. The Coles reasoned that, if the communists were using this means so widely to promote communism, why not use the same method to make the gospel known to the French masses, even if it were just a single verse of Scripture. An offer of a New Testament could be made, which would give an opportunity for personal contact. They intended to deliver the New Testaments personally, and did this whenever it was possible.

The Coles had been billposting for two years and were receiving about twenty letters a month. They were working independently and receiving just a pittance for support from their church in England. They desperately felt the need, not only for financial help, but physical help in their billposting work. It is hard work! So they decided to ask the Institute for help.

Dave arrived at the Institute at the end of a faculty prayer meeting. We five missionaries and our nine students felt very inadequate for the task of witnessing, even in our own immediate area, and in spite of our zeal and systematic efforts to cover the town of Chatou with literature, we were limited in what we could do. So the burden of our prayers that afternoon was «Lord, raise up someone with a burden to get the Word of God into the hands of French people everywhere, not only in France but in the francophone world.» And in answer to our prayers, there was Dave Cole standing before us with his request for student and financial help.

We were so impressed by Dave's sincerity, and by what God was doing through his billposting ministry, that we invited him, on the spot, to join our ranks. We still had great financial needs, but we knew God would bless and supply the finances for this vital area of our Institute ministry. We had no hesitation, therefore, in asking Dave and Pat Cole to become members of our Institute family.

Gospel billposting was a wonderful means for EBI students to witness, and they began working with the Coles in this important ministry. We teachers also went out many weekends with student teams to paste posters, distribute tracts and talk to people personally in the streets. This billposting ministry challenged other missionaries working in France, as well as many national pastors, and hundreds of thousands of posters have been sent out from the Institute all over the French-speaking world. Only eternity will reveal how many came to know Christ through this initial contact with the Word of God.

Gospel billposting was the means God used to bring a number of students to EBI. The story of one such student, Yves Perrier, French national evangelist and presently Secretary of the French Evangelical Alliance, is told in TROPHIES OF GRACE - how he was contacted by a student billposting team from EBI.

As the gospel billposting ministry grew, the need for Bible correspondence follow up was recognized and a simple four-lesson course on the Gospel of John was produced by the Navigators and used by the Institute for several years.

One day in an administration meeting, David Barnes, who had become Director of the Institute, shared a prayer burden he had on his heart. He was praying, he told us, about placing an advertisement in the *French Reader's Digest* offering a Bible to the first hundred, a New Testament to the next two hundred, and a Gospel to everyone else who might write for the offer. The whole project: the advertisement, the Scriptures, the postage, etc., would cost roughly

$2,000. We didn't have $20 in our literature fund at that time.

«Look at it this way,» Dave said. «I have been informed by the Reader's Digest that they have a paid subscription of a million and a half readers, and they figure another million more, at least, read it in libraries, hospitals, doctors and dentists' clinics, and so forth. It takes us weeks, sometimes months, to cover a small area going from door to door and at best we can only distribute a few thousand tracts. Through this advertisement we could present at least two million people with an offer of a Gospel and a correspondence course. I have also been told by Reader's Digest that a half page advertisement will bring in about 10,000 requests. Let us pray about it.»

We did pray much about this project and shared it with our missionary colleagues in the bi-monthly meeting. The funds came in and the advertisement was paid for to be inserted in the October Digest, a good month because schools would be starting and many students would be buying the Digest, so we had been informed. But it was not just students who wrote for a Bible; we received over seven thousand letters in the weeks following the insertion of the advertisement. They came from all over the French-speaking world and from every strata of society. For months, even for several years, we received requests from people who saw the advertisement for the first time.

One person in Africa had heard about it but didn't know how or where to write and simply addressed his letter, «Monsieur La Bible, France.» We still find it hard to believe that the French post office in Paris actually took the time to phone several Bible agencies, including the British and Foreign Bible Society's office in Paris, to ask how they might deliver this letter. The BFBS told them to send it to our school and the African received his Bible.

However, we had a problem that was created by our advertisement. We had hoped to be able to offer everyone a Gospel of John and the first lesson of the Navigator course on John. When we contacted the Navs, we discovered they had only a few hundred courses in print and wouldn't have another printing done for several months. We also learned that the Bible Society in Paris didn't have any Gospels of John. So I wrote to the Scripture Gift Mission of London, England, to ask for their help and advice, and told them we might need 10,000 Gospels of John. The SGM usually have an adequate supply of all their literature, but they didn't have enough Gospels of John and it would be some months before a new printing could be done. They suggested we use the Gospel of Luke and write a course based on this Gospel and they could send us 10,000 as a gift.

I was asked by the faculty to prepare this gospel course. I read through Luke several times and wherever I noted a verse or passage that emphasized the person of Christ, I underlined it in my Bible. I did the same for the word power, and *péché, pecheur* (sin, sinner) and also for the word pardon. I eventually came up with a four-lesson gospel course based on the Person of Christ, the Power of Christ, the Pecheur (sinner) before Christ, and the Pardon Christ gives. In the third lesson we included an article on «Repentance,» by D. L. Moody. We put a decision card in the fourth lesson. Of the seven thousand persons who wrote and received a Bible, New Testament or Gospel, seven hundred completed the four-lesson course. Of the seven hundred, sixty-one sent back decision cards indicating some kind of commitment to Christ.

Whenever it was possible, the converts were put in

touch with a church, or a missionary, or pastor, or in some cases with just another Christian living in the area. Many asked us for more Bible courses, which we did not have at that time. In fact, few missions were offering such courses. So for the next ten years I tried to write a Bible course each summer. When we left France in 1976, we had completed ten courses. In the following three years, spent in the Republic of Ireland, when we were free from teaching and administrative responsibilities, we added another nine courses to the curriculum. Some of these courses have been translated into nearly a score of languages and are being used on every continent in the world.

A book could easily be written about the ministry of the Personal Bible Studies, the name given to the Bible correspondence courses, how God has used them to lead hundreds to Christ. When I wrote the course on Luke, I was obliged by the religious, perhaps I should say the non-religious, nature of the correspondents who would receive the course, to make it as simple as I could. At the same time I tried to present the gospel as clearly as it is found in Luke's Gospel. I have been astonished over and over again to read letters from highly intelligent people, those in the teaching profession, for example: high school teachers, and even one professor from Brussel's University, who wrote saying, «I have made the greatest discovery of my life - to know Christ in a personal way and to have the assurance of salvation and eternal life.» I have to remind myself that I have known these simple gospel truths from my infancy, almost.

The Scripture clearly teaches in I Corinthians 2:9-14 that it is not the spirit of man that can discern and understand God's Word, but only when the Word is illuminated by the Spirit of God can one understand it. «Now we have received the spirit which is from God that we might know the things that are freely given to us of God.»

The professor in Brussels had seen a gospel bill-poster in a small store window, and wrote for a Gospel and a Bible course and, because he was hungry to know the truth, he found Christ. «You shall seek me and find me, if you seek for me with all your heart and with all your soul.» (Deuteronomy 4:29)

A high school teacher was led to Christ in the same way. He confided to a colleague that a girl who cleaned his home had been plaguing him and his wife to become Jehovah's Witnesses, and he said to his colleague, «My problem is that I do not know how to answer her questions because I don't have a Bible and have never studied one.» His friend, who knew about the gospel billposting ministry, advised him to write to EBI for a Bible and a correspondence course. He did, and received both, and was led to Christ through the Luke course. He completed all the courses and has become one of the outstanding evangelicals leaders in his city.

But the letter that moved me more than any I have read, and I have read scores of them, came from a man in the central part of France. The letter was written about eighteen months ago and here is the translation. Only his signature has been changed.

At the age of thirty I was tired of living. Life had no longer any meaning for me. I worked long, hard hours in the industrial center of my country, but it was not the hard labor that bothered me. What did bother me was that I was unhappily married and our domestic life had become unbearable. I could find no solution. My wife and I were completely incompatible. I'm sure I was as much to blame for the unhappy state of affairs as she was.

Every evening the arguments grew worse and I finally decided to end it all. It seemed the only way out. The railroad ran close by our home under a bridge, and

I kept thinking, «How easy it would be to end it all; one quick jump and my problems would be solved.» One evening I returned from work and decided to end it all. My wife was not at home, so I hastily wrote her a note and left it on the kitchen table. The note said, «At last you will be free of me; I have gone to commit suicide; goodbye for ever.»

As I approached the railroad bridge my heart was heavy. I knew the next train was due to pass in five minutes. But suddenly I noticed a poster on the wall of the bridge that someone had pasted there. My eyes fell upon it and I read these words, «Come unto me all ye that labour and are heavy laden, and I will give you rest.»

Immediately, I was attracted to the poster like a moth is attracted to light. But who is this Jesus? Ah, yes, He must be the Jesus I had heard about as a child. But what can He do for me today? I stood absolutely transfixed before this poster as if some invisible force was holding me there while the train passed under the bridge.

It was then I noticed the offer of a free Testament and a Bible course if I would write to the European Bible Institute. Yes, I must write for this Testament and find out more about Jesus. Perhaps there is still hope.

Then I remembered the suicide note I had left for my wife. What mockery I would have to endure from her when I got home and she learned that I had not committed suicide! She would treat my note like a joke and me as a coward. Nevertheless, I had to go back and face her and tell her what had happened, because the message of the poster was burning in my mind.

As I entered the house I braced myself for the worst, but strangely everything was quiet; my wife had not returned. I quickly destroyed the suicide note and wrote another note, this time to the European Bible Institute, and requested the New Testament. Several days later I received it with the first lesson on Luke's Gospel. I answered the questions, sent them back and received the second, third and fourth lessons.

The study of the New Testament became a passion. Then I received the entire Bible. Marvelous new truths were penetrating my heart and mind. But I had many problems and many questions. These I shared with my

EBI correspondent who showed me from God's Word the answers. Lesson after lesson, course after course, were completed and yet I did not experience real peace in my heart. Then one day through the study of God's Word, I suddenly realized that I had to make a personal commitment of my life to Christ and receive Him as my Saviour and Lord .It was at that moment that I truly believed and became a child of God.

I began witnessing to my friends of my new found faith in Christ. In my spare moments I went from door to door selling Bibles. Finally, I quit my work and became a Bible colporteur. I must share this message of hope with my fellow-countrymen who know not Christ. I pray also for my wife's salvation and that she will find through Christ the peace and joy I have experienced.

Rene Dubois

When I read Rene Dubois' letter just a few months ago, I was thrilled to the depths of my soul. I thought, «Praise God, it has been worth it all: the vision of the Coles and their gospel billposting ministry; Dave Barnes' burden to share the Word of God with the millions of Reader's Digest subscribers, the faithful French pastor who pasted that poster on the railroad bridge, the patience of the EBI correspondent who discipled Rene Dubois, all of these servants of God who were used in bringing this prospective suicide to a knowledge of Christ. God moves in a mysterious way His wonders to perform.»

Rene Dubois is only one of hundreds who have been led to Christ through the Bible correspondence courses. In a recent letter, Larry Sutherland, Director of the Bible Correspondence Department of the German Bible Institute in Seeheim, wrote to me, saying,

Bob, you may not agree with me, but I believe your Bible correspondence courses have contributed more to the evangelistic outreach of GBI than any other service you may have rendered to the Lord on this continent.

An average of forty persons each year send in decision cards after completing the Luke course. Thanks for what you have done to help us here at GBI.

All nineteen courses have been translated into German and are being used effectively by the German Bible Institute. Another mission in Germany called «The German Mission to Lepers and the Blind» is using all the courses in their mission work in India and West Africa. The Luke course as well as the courses on Romans, The Holy Spirit and the Person of Christ have been translated into a score of languages, including Chinese. We pray daily that God will use them for His glory.

The European Bible Institute has also been characterized for its emphasis on missions at home and abroad. While Europe may be considered one of the neediest mission fields of the world, one cannot legislate God's call to young people. The Lord did not tell us to pray that He would send forth laborers into Europe but into the harvest fields of the world. So while the Greater Europe Mission schools are training Europeans to evangelize Europeans, the motto of the European Bible Institute is «Bearing Christ to the world.» How can EBI students think of bearing Christ to the world unless they can share in a worldwide missionary vision? What better way to do this than through the auspices of the European Students Missionary Association?

I shared some of my personal burden with the EBI administration in the early years of the Institute, regarding the possibility of starting a Foreign Missions Fellowship chapter in the school. I was appointed as a committee of one and given a free hand to develop the chapter. I wrote to the FMF President in the United States and told him our desire to make FMF known in Bible schools in Europe. I received an encouraging letter from him, urging me to keep it European. He emphasized this in his letter, «Brother, keep the organization European and give it a European name. By all means use the principles and practices of FMF, but I reiterate, keep it European.» Well, I got the point and we kept it European. We called it the European Students Missionary Association. (ESMA)

When I explained the project to the EBI students they were all enthusiastic, and ESMA began that same week. A committee was formed and a Dutch student, named Joop Schotanus, was elected by the students as President of the Association. It was Joop, really, who enthused the other students in the project. He and his wife were planning to go to Africa, so he had missions upon his heart. He came to me often to share different ESMA projects and we prayed that God would use ESMA to give missionary vision and challenge to Bible school students throughout Europe. God did this in a wonderful way.

When Joop graduated he was able to postpone his military service for several months, during which time he visited a number of Bible schools to share the vision of ESMA with them. He was not too enthusiastically received as most of the schools had some kind of student missionary prayer meeting with which they were satisfied.

A year later Bill Boerop, another Dutch student, became President. Under Bill's leadership the EBI chapter of ESMA decided to hold its first foreign missionary conference. Three well-known mission leaders in England were invited for the weekend conference. Invitations were sent to a number of Bible schools in Europe and the British Isles. EBI students offered to pay half the expenses of any student coming to the conference from outside France. This was a big step of faith and a practice carried on for a few years until it became impossible. It was sometimes abused by visiting students who added all kinds of expenses to their travel tickets!

Only three students came from another Bible Institute in France, which was very disappointing. But the conference was not a disappointment. It was a tremendous success and EBI students at the end of the conference enthusiastically voted to have an annual missionary conference whether other students came or not. They took up an offering for the visiting speakers which came to 20,001 francs, about $500 at the current rate of exchange. This amazed us because more than half of the students were trying to work their way through school and had very little spare money. Someone joked about the odd franc. However, in order to divide the offering evenly between the three speakers, the odd franc was needed. Each received 6667 francs!

Pastor Andre Thobois, President of the French Baptist Federation and teacher for many years at EBI, attended several of the meetings during the conference. He was thrilled by what he saw and heard and asked the ESMA committee if the next conference could be held in his church in Paris, as he wished to expose his members to the missionary vision of ESMA.

At the second missionary conference twenty students from other schools attended and the second conference was even better than the first. That was the first and last time that an ESMA conference was held in a local church. Next year it moved to Emmaus Bible Institute in Lausanne, Switzerland; the third year it moved to the German Bible Institute, then over to London Bible College, and back again to EBI and then up to the Belgian Bible Institute in Heverlee. Each year for the past two decades an ESMA chapter in a different Bible school has been responsible for the annual conference. The con-

196

ference became so big and so popular among students that it was decided to have two conferences each year, one for northern Europe and one for southern Europe.

Eric Gay came to EBI from Switzerland to study for one year before joining Gospel Recordings as an experienced electronics engineer. At the end of his first year of study, he decided to stay a second year, and then a third. Eric was elected President of ESMA and under his direction the conference was organized and held again at EBI. It was the largest conference yet held in a Bible school, with five hundred students attending and about fifty missions represented. Eric and his committee did a tremendous job of organizing this conference. ESMA is organized and all its activities conducted by students, with a faculty advisor at each school. During that conference God gave Eric a vision. It was obvious that no one school could handle the number of students now coming. Eric thought, «Why not have a larger conference, not only for Bible school students but for young people from Christian organizations, such as Youth for Christ, Campus Crusade for Christ, The Navigators, The Torchbearers, and students from non-Christian universities and colleges? Why not let young people who are not students share in this missionary vision and challenge?»

Eric graduated from EBI and travelled around some of the Bible schools in Europe and England as Joop had done twenty years before. This time students everywhere were enthusiastic about the possibility of a European «Urbana» type of conference. Eric formed a committee, mostly made up of EBI graduate students, and they held their first Europe-wide missionary conference in Lausanne in 1976 and called it MISSION 76. Three thousand students attended, with fifty to sixty mission representatives.

Four years later 7,000 attended MISSION 80, along with two hundred missionaries. Four years from now, if another conference is held, it could double again.

The tri-lingual secretary of EBI, who attended the conference as an interpreter, wrote me the following letter.

Dear Mr. Munn:

I wish you had been able to share in this unforgettable conference that was MISSION 80. During the Mission our thoughts were turned to you in America. At noontime we had a meeting with EBI alumni and present students. We were 70 in number. Joop Schotanus told us all about the beginning of ESMA and, of course, you were mentioned.

The Lord has really blessed since that small ESMA conference in EBI twenty years ago. Now there were 7,000 gathered at MISSION 80, including many missionaries. There were 200 missionary booths. EBI and the other GEM schools were represented at these booths. We gave our catalogue to many interested young people. It was a blessing to all of us to see what God is doing.

Ruth Nussbaumer

Yes, it is a blessing to see what God is doing in the lives of young people throughout the world. It is not this kind of young people who make the headlines in today's media, just the terrorists, the drug addicts and other delinquents. But God is moving in the hearts of young people everywhere and these are «the leaven that leaveneth the whole lump.» These are «the salt of the earth» and «the light of the world.» These young people are the future of world evangelization before the Lord returns. «Lift up your eyes and look on the fields for they are white unto harvest.» «Lift up your hands and pray.» «Lift up your feet and go.» These are Biblical commands given by Christ and the apostle Paul. And Jesus also said, «If you love me, you will keep my commandments,» and «Why do you call me Lord and do not the things which I say?»

So in a brief twenty-five years the European Bible Institute, which began with five missionaries and nine students, has grown into a large mission, the Greater Europe Mission. The school became the center of evangelism. Through its students, its Christian service outreach, its French evangelistic team, its gospel billposting ministry, its radio programs, its Bible correspondence courses and, last but not least, its worldwide missionary emphasis through ESMA, it influences not only the evangelization of Europe, but reaches to the uttermost part of the earth. God has been pleased to use EBI as a sharp threshing instrument for the extension of His kingdom.

In the early years EBI was criticized by some as being a school of evangelism and missions but not having any theological program. This criticism was not altogether true. Evangelism and missions? Yes. Not having a theological program? Decidedly not true. Every teacher who has taught at EBI has had under-graduate or post-graduate degrees in theology and languages from some of the best known theological schools and universities in the USA and Europe. The criticism was gladly accepted, however, because the goal of the Greater Europe Mission is «Training Europeans to *Evangelize* Europeans.» What better way to evangelize than by preaching the gospel in all its simplicity so that people can understand the message, believe and be saved. Many hundreds have been saved through the European Bible Institute and its sister schools throughout Europe.

Our struggles to get EBI established were many, but the grace of God was always abundant and His provision for every need at our disposal. The only thing God cannot do is fail! It was Jeremiah who wrote under the inspiration of God's Spirit words that have been a comfort and strength to believers in every generation and in every circumstance. «It is of the Lord's mercies that we are not consumed, because his compassions fail not. They are new every morning. Great is thy faithfulness.» (Lamentations 3:20-23)

When we left Europe in 1976 to work in the Republic of Ireland, we could look back and thank God for the way He had led us. It was a perfect way. It was a way of faith. It was a way of blessing. We will always feel grateful to God for the privilege He gave us to have a spiritual influence in the lives of so many young people. They came to EBI from all over western Europe, as well as from many lands overseas. Some of their ministries are told in the tenth chapter of this book. To God and to God alone be all the praise and glory, for he alone is worthy.

CHAPTER 10

Training Timothys

> And the things that thou hast heard of me among many witnesses, the same commit thou to faithful men who shall be able to teach others, also.
>
> (II Timothy 2:2)

Missionary multiplication? A spiritual chain reaction? A divine principle for world evangelization? Discipling Timothys? Call it what you will, but the apostle Paul, inspired by the Holy Spirit, commanded Timothy to continue the ministry that had been committed to the early disciples by Christ Himself, when He commanded them, «Go ye therefore and teach (make disciples of) all nations...teaching them to observe all things whatsoever I have commanded you....» (Matthew 28:19-20)

It is very significant that the Acts of the Apostles begins with the statement, «The former treatise have I made, O Theophilos, of all that Jesus *began* to do and to teach.» What Christ had begun He was going to continue through His disciples. Mark, in the closing chapter of his Gospel, reiterates this divine principle: «And they went forth and preached everywhere, the *Lord working with them,* and confirming the word with signs following. Amen.» (Mark 16:20)

This ministry of *doing* and *teaching* was nothing less than a continuation of Christ's ministry from heaven through the apostles' ministry on earth. Paul was conscious of this same truth from the very beginning of his missionary career. He recognized that he was a worker together *with* Christ. (II Corinthians 6:1) When he returned from his first missionary journey, accompanied by Barnabas, it is recorded of them in Acts 14:27, «And when they were come (to Antioch) and had gathered the church together, they rehearsed all that God had done *with* them, and how he had opened the door of faith unto the Gentiles.»

In the same manner Christ, before going to the cross to die, committed the continuation of His ministry to His apostles, (As the Father hath sent me, even so send I you.) Paul, likewise, as he was about to lay down his life for Christ, committed the continuation of his ministry to young Timothy. «And the things that thou hast heard of me among many witnesses, the same commit thou to faithful men who shall be able to teach others also.» God buries His workmen but carries on his work. Hallelujah!

During our twenty-five years of ministry on the continent of Europe we had the privilege of helping to train nearly four hundred young people who came from thirty different countries, eighty per cent of whom, today, are serving Christ and being used by the Holy Spirit to win many souls for Christ. The stories of some of these men and women of God, such as Jean Herrgott from Alsace, George Papadopoulos from Greece, Yves and Francoise Perrier from France, John Dewerse from Belgium, Alain Auceps and Meta Knecht from Holland, and others, have been told in «TROPHIES OF GRACE.»

When I began to write this book I had no particular plan concerning the chapter titles, but have simply recorded the way that God has led me and my wife these many years. It seemed incomplete, however, to write about the European Bible Institute without mentioning some more of its graduates, where they are and what God is doing through them. When I wrote and asked them to share with me some of the fruits of their ministry and God's direction in their lives, I have been thrilled and humbled to have had a part in their preparation for the work of the Lord.

The motto of the Greater Europe Mission, «Training Europeans to Evangelize Europeans,» is Biblical and it works. This Biblical principle has been exemplified in the lives of many of the graduates of EBI, as well as other GEM sponsored schools. It is a «continuing ministry.» It is «reproducers producing reproducers.» It is a «spiritual chain reaction» and only the Lord knows where it will end. Here is an account of the ministries of some of the EBI «Timothys.»

THE BURKLIN TRIO: Germany and the USA

It is rare to find all the children of the same family studying at the same time in the same Bible school, but this was true of the Burklins. The Burklin Trio, as the students called them, left a deep impression and vibrant testimony at the European Bible Institute. Endowed with many gifts they could say with the Psalmist, «...we have a goodly heritage.» (Psalm 16:6)

Fred, Werner and Joy were born in China. Their parents were German missionaries with the China Inland Mission (now called Overseas Missionary Fellowship). They attended a German public school in Shanghai while their parents worked in the interior in Kiangsi Province. During World War II they were separated from their parents for five years.

«We tried to keep in touch with Dad and Mom,» Fred said. «As teenagers we had problems that we longed to share with them. We often wrote for their advice but it took weeks, sometimes months, for answers to come back, by which time the whole situation had changed. It was very frustrating.»

It is hard to understand what this separation meant to both parents and children. Only those who have passed through a similar experience can understand the pain, the sense of helplessness and futility that one feels at such times. But God was good to them and Mr. and Mrs. Burklin never ceased to pray that God would keep His hand upon their children, bring them to a saving knowledge of Christ and call them into His service. Their prayers were to be abundantly answered, and in spite of internment, separation and anxiety, they experienced the peace of God which passes all understanding.

The war ended and British and American missionaries were released from Japanese internment camps. Mr. and Mrs. Burklin, however, continued to be interned by the Chinese, and were kept under house arrest on their mission compound. CIM missionaries and others began evangelistic meetings again in Shanghai. The three Burklin children started to attend youth meetings held in the Evangelical Free Church, and Fred tells his impression of these meetings.

«What impressed me most was the way the young people sang so happily and so enthusiastically, something I had never heard or seen before. I recall one Sunday morning when I was waiting outside the church for the communion service to finish, an elderly gentleman approached me and asked me this simple question, 'Young man, are you saved?' My parents were missionaries; I attended church services regularly; I never doubted the existence of God, the reality of Jesus Christ or the validity of God's revealed Word. To my knowledge, however, no one had ever asked me this question directly and I had never knowingly committed my life to Jesus Christ.

«I responded, 'Yes, I know I am saved.' I was on the spot and had to give him an answer, but I believe that my conversion experience dates from that moment of confession, based on Romans 10:9-10, 'That if thou shalt confess with thy mouth the Lord Jesus and believe in thine heart that God hath raised him from the dead, thou shalt be saved. For with the heart man believeth unto righteousness and with the mouth confession is made unto salvation.' I suddenly had the assurance that I was truly a child of God and since that time, as a youth of seventeen years, I have never doubted my salvation. It was about the same time that my brother, Werner, and my sister Joy, also must have come to know the Saviour.»

In 1946 the three young people finally got permission from the Chinese government to visit their parents in Kiangsi. They left Shanghai in June; the sun was shining and their hearts were filled with joy and excitement at the prospects of the reunion with Dad and Mom. Vivid in Fred's memory is the three-day boat trip up the river in a Chinese junk. The boat swarmed with passengers from bow to stern. At night the young people made the acquaintance of other «Chinese millions» which suddenly appeared from the mattresses after dark! But the bedbugs did not dampen their enthusiasm. The only momentary disappointment came when the Mission Superintendent was obliged to return to Shanghai and leave the young people to finish the journey alone.

Fred had forgotten much of the Chinese language he had known, except for a few phrases to buy food and ask for directions. After the boat trip there were two days of traveling in an old bus which brought them to the town where their parents lived. News of their coming had not reached the mission compound so no one was at the bus station to meet them.

«I called several coolies,» Fred said, «and told them to take our luggage to the Jesus Hall, hoping they would know where it was. They did and immediately started out, leading us through narrow streets and alleys and finally stopping at the compound. We knocked loudly on the door and heard someone bestirring himself inside. Slowly the door opened and there stood our Chinese cook, whom we had not seen for years. He turned on his heels, leaving us standing at the door, and ran towards the house yelling at the top of his lungs, 'The children are here; the children are here.'

«We entered the compound and Father was the first to meet us. We all felt a little strange and I asked my father in a rather businesslike way if he would take care of the carriers and pay them for their service. Then Mother came running out of the house and flung herself into our arms. It was a happy reunion after five years of separation.

Fred continued his story. «The first thing Father did was to lead us to the veranda where a number of Bible picture posters were hanging on the wall. He used these to explain the gospel and teach the Bible to the servants and visitors who came to the house, because at that time many Chinese were illiterate. He took several of the posters and began to explain them to us as if we also were illiterate! In very simple language he told us the gospel story. All this before he had asked us any news about ourselves or friends in Shanghai or anything. Then he asked each one of us in turn, 'Do you know the Lord Jesus Christ as your personal Saviour?' Strangely enough, until that particular moment, none of us had ever confessed our faith to one another. But each of us answered Father in the affirmative. Certainly, this must have been a very special day for our parents to hear the confession of faith of their children and to know that their prayers had been answered.»

Later, Fred, Werner and Joy were baptized in a Chinese church by a Chinese elder and their father. They remained with their parents for a year, after which time Werner and Joy returned to Shanghai to continue their education, while Fred stayed on with his parents because he could not get any higher education at the time. He was asked by the local Chinese high school to teach English to the upper classes, which he did with much pleasure. This enabled him to learn many of the Chinese characters and he began to find it easy to converse with the students; in fact, he learned Chinese well enough to be able to preach in it.

Fred accompanied his father on a number of gospel itineraries. As they went from village to village, on foot, sharing in the life of the common people, and preaching the gospel to them, Fred began to feel more and more that God was calling him to be a missionary. On one such gospel trip he surrendered his life to Christ for missionary service.

«Along the mountain path we were traveling,» Fred recalls, «there were countless villages off the beaten track that we could never possibly visit and often I wondered, 'How will they ever hear the gospel?' The text that repeatedly came to my mind during that particular trip was Romans 10:14, 'How then shall they call on him in whom they have not believed, and how shall they believe in him of whom they have not heard, and how shall they hear without a preacher?' It was through this passage that God began to speak to my own heart about serving Him as a foreign missionary. I dedicated my life to a teaching ministry, if God would some day make this possible, and thank God He did make it possible. Praise God!»

It was thirteen years before Fred's call became a reality, when he returned to Germany to teach at the German Bible Institute in Seeheim. Before he arrived there, however, there were years of discipline to be experienced and a theological education to be acquired. Fred enrolled in Grace College and later in Grace Seminary, where he received his M.Div. magna cum laud. More graduate work followed in Westminister Theological Seminary, where he received his Th.M. At Grace College Fred met Joyce Austin, a Hoosier from Lagrange, and they were married while Fred was still a student in Grace Seminary. The Burklins arrived at Seeheim in 1961, where Fred has carried a major teaching load, besides filling a number of administrative positions at GBI.

«The reason I returned to Europe was very simple,» Fred told me. «China had become a closed country and Germany had wide open doors. Besides, it is the land of my mother tongue and the opportunity to teach at the German Bible Institute was accepted by Joyce and me as God's will for our lives. And His will is 'good and perfect and *acceptable*.'»

Werner was the restless one of the trio. How bored he used to get with the long meetings! In one particular worship service, he became so bored with the pastor's long sermon that he walked out of the church and waited for the service to finish. An old missionary with a long white beard approached him and asked him if he knew Christ as his personal Saviour. Like Fred, it was the first time anyone had ever asked Werner that question. It was undoubtedly the same old faithful missionary who had talked with Fred.

«His question really bothered me,» said Werner, «and three or four days later I knelt down by my bed and asked Christ to come into my life.»

Werner went to Germany in 1949, to a Germany that had been ravaged and torn by war. It was hard to forget China, the land where his parents had spent twenty-five years with only one furlough! From time to time Werner felt that God was calling him also to be a missionary, but the years of separation from his parents, as well as the frustrations of growing up in a foreign culture and many other things began to cloud his missionary vision. His uncle, a successful businessman, invited Werner to work for him and carry on his business after he would retire.

«It was a terrific temptation for me,» Werner said. «I liked my uncle very much and his business interested me immensely. I knew I could make money and live well and have a good time from a worldly and material point of view. But all the time there was this nagging conviction that God wanted me in fulltime Christian work. Sometimes I would argue with myself and say, 'Well, supposing I go to China or some other mission field, I'm only one person, whereas if I become a successful businessman, I can support ten missionaries.' But the Lord seemed to keep telling me, 'Werner, I want *you,* not your money.

«While this struggle was going on in my heart, I received a wonderful letter from Bishop Houghton, Director of the China Inland Mission. The good bishop kept in touch with many of the CIM missionary children all over the world, assuring them that he was praying for them and urging them to stay close to the Saviour. I believe it was Bishop Houghton's letter that had much to do with my decision to enter God's service. Also I had come into contact with Rev. Bob Hopkins, Director of the Navigators in Germany. It was he who told me about Bob Evans and the European Bible Institute and advised me to get in touch with Dr. Evans. However, I had plans to go to the USA to spend a year working in a youth organization, so I didn't write to Dr. Evans at that time.

After arriving in the United States Werner received a letter from Bob Evans' mother telling him that she, too, was praying for him that he might know God's will and a short time later he received a letter from Bob Evans also telling him the same thing.

It would have been comparatively easy for Werner to have stayed in the United States. He spoke English fluently and a scholarship could have been easily obtained.

«But I am European,» Werner said, «and somehow I felt that the training I would receive at the European Bible Institute would better prepare me to work among my fellow Europeans. So I decided to go to EBI.»

I recently asked Werner to share with me how God led him in his present ministry and what the Lord has been doing *with* him and this is what he said. «In Shanghai I first came into touch with Youth for Christ. It was through the preaching of Dr. Bob Pierce, at that time a YFC evangelist, that I dedicated my life to fulltime Christian service at a YFC rally in Shanghai.

»During the summer months at EBI I returned to Germany as a youth evangelist, preaching all over the country. I started a Youth For Christ rally in Frankfurt which grew from 600 to 2,000 in attendance and at every rally we saw young people accept Christ. I meet people all the time in different parts of Germany and overseas who tell me they found Christ as their Saviour, or they dedicated their lives to Christ, at the Frankfurt rallies.

»Later I directed the total ministry of Germany Youth for Christ, then became European Director of YFC. In the late sixties I left Germany with my family and spent a year in Jamaica, where we organized Youth for Christ in that island, and today the YFC work is still going strong there with its own staff and financial support.

»Since 1977 I have been director for Outreach Ministries for Youth for Christ International on a worldwide basis. We had the privilege of planning and directing the largest youth congress ever held in Brazil. Other such discipleship training congresses are being planned for other countries as well.

»Besides my ministry with Youth for Christ, I also direct the Billy Graham Evangelistic Association in Europe. The hearts of young people are open to the gospel in an unprecedented way, especially in Europe, I feel. What we have seen in the last two or three years gives me tremendous courage to go ahead and believe for great things. God is alive and working! In Youth for Christ we are now involved in evangelistic outreach all across the world. I don't know how things will turn out, eventually, but I want to be involved up to the hilt in evangelism and discipleship training.»

Some years ago when I was talking with Werner on one of his visits to EBI, he said to me, «Mr. Munn, my ministry in Youth for Christ is simply an extension of the ministry of EBI. I am seeking to share with young people what I learned among many witnesses at the Institute, that they might be able to teach others also.»

Joy was the last but not the least of the Burklin Trio. Her Chinest name is She-loh, which translated means Joy. Joy has lived up to her name. Her love for the Saviour is real; her joy in sharing her faith with others is contagious. A gifted linguist, speaking Chinese, French, German, Dutch and English, she has shared her joy in all of these languages. When she was sixteen years old she was regularly featured on a children's program, broadcast in Shanghai, until the communists closed down the station.

Fred, Werner and Joy often sang as a trio at EBI and while Fred has become primarily involved in a teaching ministry and Werner in evangelistic work, Joy continues to share her faith in song and testimony.

While at EBI Joy met and fell in love with Bill Boerop who was born in The Netherlands. When Bill was seventeen years old, his father, a businessman, joined the Christian Literature Crusade and the Boerop family went to Belgium as missionaries. For five years before going to EBI, Bill was already involved in missionary work in Belgium. When he arrived at EBI he was sold on missions and during his student days at the Institute Bill played an important role in the development of the European Students Missionary Association.

Bill for many years was the Southeastern Area Director of Greater Europe Mission, and as such was called upon to speak in missionary conferences and pastors' retreats, youth retreats and civic clubs, as well as preaching in hundreds of churches throughout the southeast. The work of Greater Europe Mission, in general, and of EBI in particular, has been enriched and strengthened by prayer, finances and missionary candidates through the ministry of Bill and Joy Boerop.

Mr. Burklin, Sr., has been called home to be with Christ and has joined that «great cloud of witnesses» and, who knows, perhaps he is watching, with joy and satisfaction, his children running with patience the race that is set before them. How fitting for the Burklins are the words of the apostle Paul written to another young servant of Christ:

> When I call to remembrance the unfeigned faith that is in thee, which first dwelt in thy grandmother, Lois, and thy mother, Eunice, and I am persuaded that in thee also.
> Wherefore I put thee in remembrance that thou stir up the gift of God which is in thee.

> (II Timothy 1:5-6)

*****

ROY HARRISON   Northern Ireland and Europe

During a decade of its history a number of Irish young people came to study at the European Bible Institute for the purpose of working with Child Evangelism Fellowship in Europe. Among them were Roy and Ruth Harrison.

At the tender age of eight years Roy felt his need of the Saviour. «But no one in my family or among my friends seemed to realize that I wanted to be saved,» he said. «Instead I grew up and associated with evil companions, who encouraged me in a life of sin. My brother and Mother were converted when I was fifteen years old and they began to pray for my salvation and God heard and answered their prayers.

»I entered university, still unsaved, but under conviction of sin. I began for the first time in my life to realize how empty and purposeless my life really

213

was without Christ. For several hours, one evening, I struggled with the Holy Spirit's conviction and finally I gave in. On my knees I asked Jesus to come into my heart and cleanse me from all sin. At the same time I surrendered my life to Him and to His service. I soon discovered the truth of II Corinthians 5:17. 'If any man be in Christ he is a new creation, old things are passed away and behold all things are become new.'

»I was anxious to serve the Lord and remembered how much, as a child, I wished to be saved with no one telling me how. I became immediately involved in young people's work, speaking at children's meetings, teaching in Sunday School and witnessing on every occasion to young people, winning some of them to Christ. It was with this sense of call to work among children, especially in Europe, that I enrolled as a student at the European Bible Institute.»

When I asked Roy to share with me some of his experiences as a student and as a fulltime worker with CEF in Europe, this is what he wrote:

Dear Mr. Munn:

To answer the questions in your recent letter, here is the information you requested.

What EBI meant to me: The three years I spent at the Institute were vital in preparing me for my present ministry. Four great blessings that I experienced as a student stand out in my memory. I am sure that what I will say must also be the testimony of many other EBI graduates.

1) *A THOROUGH GROUNDING IN THE WORD OF GOD:*
   I thank God for the faithful teachers who led us into a deeper knowledge and love for the Word of God.

2) *A MISSIONARY VISION:*
   Through participation in the Students Missionary Association I received a vision for missionary work worldwide which I shall never forget.

3) *EXPERIENCE IN CHRISTIAN SERVICE:*

It was a tremendous experience to be able to put into practice what we learned in the classroom. Every aspect of the Christian service program prepared me for my work with CEF, door-to-door evangelism, tract distribution, children's work, personal evangelism and visiting churches in teams. What a wonderful preparation was ours at EBI!

4) *FELLOWSHIPPING WITH STUDENTS FROM MANY DIFFERENT COUNTRIES:*

What a privilege it was for me to study in a bilingual and multi-racial school, to live with students from different cultures and different church backgrounds, and to learn to appreciate them and see Christ in them. What lessons we learned from one another as we lived according to the truth, «You are all One in Christ.»

You asked me to share with you some of the fruits of our ministry in Child Evangelism Fellowship. At least three of the children we led to the Lord in the early days of our ministry in France are now in fulltime Christian service. Also as the result of one of the Good News Clubs we helped to get started, a local church has begun in that area, where previously there was none. This church has three Good News Clubs as part of its outreach ministry.

During the past six years Ruth and I have been assigned to promote the literature program of CEF. Over seventy different books, tracts and visualized aids, etc., have been produced for CEF, Europe. Our latest productions are a book called «The Responsibility of Christian Parents» and a series of doctrinal lessons called «What Every Child Ought to Know.» This literature is being used by CEF in twenty-four European countries. What a wonderful privilege is ours to be ambassadors of Christ to the children of Europe.

Roy and *Ruth Harrison.*

*****

JEAN ISCH   France and Canada

Jean was one of the Parisians who came to EBI. Born into a non-Christian home, he lost his mother while still a little boy. His father showed no interest in his family and left his children to the care of his mother. The grandmother tried her best to raise the children in a religious atmosphere but until the age of twenty Jean knew nothing of the gospel.

«When I was eighteen years old,» he said, «in order to get away from my family I joined the French marines. At the end of one year I was invalided out of the service. For several years I tried one job after another without success. I was restless and constantly troubled with questions for which I could find no answers. I often wondered what life held for me. I was without Christ and without hope. What to do? I didn't know and no one seemed to be able to tell me.

»One day, at the insistence of my sister, I went with her to a young people's meeting in a gospel hall near where we lived. I was very impressed with their sincerity and their joy and I talked with the pastor, an English missionary, about some of my doubts and fears. He was a patient, gentle and serious person and it was he who enabled me to understand the gospel and accept Christ.

»What a revelation it was for me to discover that Jesus was the Son of God, that He died for my sins on the cross of Calvary, and that by accepting Him as my Saviour I would receive eternal life. When I learned all this, there was nothing less I could do than accept Him as my Saviour and Lord.

»However, this did not happen all at once. For nearly a year I resisted His love and then one night alone in my bedroom I got down on my knees, and I think for the first time in my life I prayed a spontaneous prayer. My first words were, 'Lord, you have won, I come to you as a sinner and I receive your gift of eternal life.'

»Not long after my conversion I learned that there

was a monthly youth meeting held at the European Bible Institute. I attended and was impressed by the kindness of the teachers and the contagious enthusiasm of the students. The whole atmosphere was spiritually uplifting and I seldom missed attending this monthly meeting.

»The more I attended the EBI meetings, the more I became convinced that God wanted me in His service. I spoke to my pastor about my desire to enter Bible School and he very wisely tried not to influence me to go to any particular school and mentioned several schools to me. However, I had become acquainted with EBI and was impressed by their Bible courses, as well as their Christian service program; also the international flavor of the school pleased me very much.

»So I entered EBI to prepare myself for whatever ministry the Lord might have in store for me. That was in 1959 and for the first time in my life I realized how little I knew of the Bible, practically nothing!

»What a new world life at EBI was for me: the discipline of the studies, the classroom lectures, the communal life of fifteen different nationalities, the Christian service assignments; every moment of every day fully occupied with some task. The weeks and months flew by and I was aware that I was growing in the grace of Christ and knowledge of the Word of God.

»At the beginning I had difficulty following some of the lectures. Because of Mr. Munn's manner of speaking quickly and covering so much of the Bible in his doctrine courses, I found it hard to follow the rhythm at times! But the systematic Bible doctrine course planted my feet firmly upon the Word of God, and I began to be able to give a reason for the hope that lies within me. I not only learned to study the

217

Bible, but to memorize it and use it to develop and grow in my Christian life.

»One thing I did quickly learn at EBI was that the courses were not theoretical but practical. They prepared me for several years of church planting and pastoral work in France, not to mention our radio ministry with ELWA, Liberia, as well as our evangelistic outreach in West Africa and now in Canada.

»One other aspect of life at EBI was the exposure to the missionary vision that was constantly before us. How could one live in such a missionary atmosphere without being affected by it? In looking back over my student days at EBI I can testify that the time given to ESMA had a fourfold influence on me:

1) To maintain a missionary vision in whatever ministry the Lord might lead me.

2) To pray consistently and intelligently for missionary work.

3) To give systematically and regularly to the work of missions.

4) Above all, I learned that the field is the world and I should be ready to offer myself to serve Christ anywhere He might lead me.»

Jean met Soula, one of the several lovely Greek girls who came to EBI. Raised in a pastor's home, endowed with a beautiful soprano voice, a gifted linguist, an excellent speaker, Soula was certainly God's gift to Jean! They make a wonderful team. After seven years in France in pastoral work they spent two terms of service with the Sudan Interior Mission, first of all in the French department of Radio ELWA in Liberia and later working among educated Africans in Benin, West Africa.

The Sudan Interior Mission requested the Isches to return to France in order to work among the thousands of Africans now living in France, as well as to represent the Mission in French-speaking Europe. Each summer for many years Jean and Soula have also ministered to the evangelical churches in Greece, challenging them with the spiritual needs of other countries besides Greece. Recently, the SIM asked Jean and Soula to represent the Mission in French Canada where they have a fruitful ministry in both Greek and French churches in the province of Quebec. At the end of two years they expect to return to continue their ministry in France. Here is a recent letter from Soula, dated March 1980:

Dear Mr. and Mrs. Munn:

We think of you often; you know you have marked our lives. Jean quotes you often, Mr. Munn, as he teaches at the Bethel Bible Institute outside Montreal. He remembers what a help you were to him twenty years ago.

He has the same attitude with his young students. He loves teaching and missed it when we were in Africa. By the way, we had a wonderful missionary conference at Bethel two weeks ago. We found great interest among the students. We were able to share the spiritual needs of Africa, France, Belgium and Greece with them. We try to share our own missionary burden with them and the Lord is blessing.

Please continue to pray for our ministry in the churches, in camps and at Bethel Bible Institute. The Lord has brought us here at a crucial moment when young people are getting converted by the dozens. Some of the church leaders seem to be afraid to speak about the needs of the world but the Lord is opening the eyes of many.

Our ministry among the French speaking and Greek churches is growing and we thank the Lord for many open doors to preach the gospel and teach God's Word, and challenge young people to commit their lives to Christ. This latter part of our ministry is most important. We pray for you often.

Your grateful students,

Soula and *Jean*

*****

SAMUEL LIBERECK   Belgium

When I wrote to Samuel to ask him to tell me how God had intervened in his life and what the Lord has been doing with him, he wrote me the following letter:

Dear Mr. Munn:

To answer the questions in your letter I will just go ahead and talk about myself! How funny it will sound to me and, whether you use my testimony or not, here it is.

I was converted in Belgium where I had come to live with my parents just before World War II began. We could not return to England and were trapped in Belgium for the duration of the war. I was often homesick for England and wished I could return.

When a Youth for Christ team visited Belgium after the war, I went to hear them because I knew they would be singing and preaching in English. Both of my parents were Christians and had been praying much for me and it was in answer to their prayers that I found Christ in that YFC meeting. I was converted in September 1951, the same month that you arrived in France to help Mr. Evans establish the European Bible Institute.

Two weeks later in the same YFC campaign under the tent, I dedicated my life to fulltime Christian service. I wanted immediately to go to Bible school, but the wise elders in my assembly restrained me, and I waited patiently until they felt that I had the spiritual maturity to enter the disciplined life of a Bible Institute.

Because of my contact with Youth for Christ and other European Christians, I felt I should study at the European Bible Institute. Then Mr. Evans came to Liege and my conversation with him confirmed by decision to go to EBI.

How can I put into a few words all the lessons I learned at EBI? I learned, first of all, what it meant to be a dedicated Christian, and I was able to grasp the good Bible teaching because of my home and church where the Bible was taught.

I think one of the greatest lessons I learned at the Institute was to trust God to meet all my needs. These included finances. I only had enough money to pay for my first term. My needs also included learning to live together with so many different nationalities. What a cosmopolitan family we were! Dutch, German, Lebanese, French, Syrian, Spanish, Swiss, Austrian, mixed up with American and Canadian teachers. What lessons we had to learn from the different cultures, and to tolerate and appreciate them. We not only learned to live with one another but to love one another sincerely. I still remember nights of prayer that some of us spent together.

The Bible and related courses profited me at maximum level. They were practical and every class for me was a «chapel» service. The teachers were leaders, inspirers and they made the Bible come alive to us. My best course was the systematic Bible doctrine course and that is still the memory I cherish most.

You will remember that most of my Christian service was done in collaboration with Mr. Dan Feryance of the Baptist Mid-Missions, helping him to establish a church in the communist town of St. Dennis. What an unforgettable experience that was to preach the gospel in a communist community, but we saw a number converted and a local church established. These are «the saints in Caesar's household.»

I sometimes smile at the sermons I tried to preach on weekend teams. My greatest thrill was to see, for the first time in my life, a man accept Christ at the end of my message. And how can I ever forget the annual St. Nicolas' Fair in Evreux when for hours, we stood on the street, in the midst of hundreds of people, singing, yelling, shouting the gospel above the noise and din of merchants and artisans all around us. And the preaching assignments you sent us on, and accompanied us to see that we did it properly! They were great and wonderful days.

I must confess that it was at EBI that I received a missionary vision. ESMA had not yet been formed but scores of missionaries stopped by to visit and speak in chapel. Your own stories of your experiences in Africa and elsewhere, when you often told us that it was only a heap of teaching notes and the Will of God for you to be in France that separated you from Africa. We felt missions in you and Miss Bonjour and Mr. Evans and Mr. Feryance and Mr. Cole and the burden of the

221

latter two for France. I believe it was important to have teachers with missionary experience and it just rubbed off on us whether we wanted it or not

After my graduation I spent several years with Mid-Missions working in Paris, Dijon and Bordeaux. Then I joined the Hour of Revival and for seven years was the manager for Dr. Eric Hutchings' evangelistic campaigns in Britain, Belgium, France and Denmark.

As our children grew older and because I was constantly away from home, I felt I needed a more settled ministry. The Lord impressed upon our hearts the need of Belgium, my adopted country, and one of Europe's neediest mission fields. I was raised in Belgium, converted in Belgium, found my wife in Belgium and now I felt the Lord was calling me to work in Belgium.

Denise and I accepted a missionary post in a small church of the old Belgian Gospel Mission. It became independent and under our leadership God has been pleased to bless the work. In recent years we joined The United World Mission. Our church has been able to start two other churches that now have their own pastor. Although we are still small in number, our missionary budget for the past year was over $8,000. More than half of our budget goes to Missions. Where did we get our missionary vision? At EBI.

Besides my pastoral work I have had the privilege of interpreting for many of God's servants who come to Europe: Billy Graham, Dr. Oswald Smith, Dr. Bob Jones, Dr. Eric Hutchings, George Verwer and others. Our daughter has graduated from EBI and teaches Bible in the Belgian school system. Our son Dan has graduated from Columbia Bible College and expects to work in Belgium as a missionary.

We praise the Lord for you and we love you!

Yours in Christ,

Sam and *Denise Libereck*

*****

JOSEPH WENGER   Alsace, France

MAURICE SEAUVE   Paris, France

The two following stories are an example of the way God is using some of the graduates of EBI to witness to their fellow-Europeans and establish local churches in their own communities. First, Joseph Wenger's story.

I was converted in 1966 through the Billy Graham Association film, «The Restless Ones.» Having no knowledge of the Bible, God, Jesus Christ or the Holy Spirit, I felt a profound need to learn more. I was directed to the European Bible Institute at Lamorlaye, where I spent two years studying God's Word. It was there I met my wife Valerie, a student from England.

After I left EBI I felt a precise leading from the Lord to work with the Billy Graham Association, presenting the Association films all over France. My aim was to evangelize by this method.

In 1969 the Association sent me to eastern France. I had not intended to create a church in Jebsheim where we lived. However, in 1973, I organized a campfire meeting in our village and invited a singing group to come and present a program of gospel music with the purpose of witnessing to the young people in Jebsheim. A good number turned up for the meeting and several showed real interest in the things of the Lord. Their plea was, «Tell us more about God.»

From that moment, in my spare time, we gathered these young people together in our home to instruct them in God's Word and explain more clearly the way of salvation. A number of them accepted Christ as their Saviour and Lord.

They began to attend the Lutheran church in the village and participated in the various activities of the church. My wife taught in the Sunday School and several of the girls helped.

Everything changed, however, upon the arrival of a new pastor. This man did not believe in the forgiveness of sins, the assurance of salvation, eternal life and many other fundamentals of the Christian faith. During a meeting of the church council, the pastor (for whom we pray regularly) asked us to leave the church and go our own way.

We decided to take the young people to an evangelical church forty-five miles away, whose pastor is Jean Herrgott, an EBI graduate. We continued to hold Bible studies, prayer meetings and evangelistic meetings in our home, which were directed by the young people with the help of older Christians from Jean's church.

Some older people joined our group and we felt the time had come to call a full time pastor. My work as an evangelist did not permit me to be present very often. We prayed and asked the Lord to show us His servant. After two years of praying and patiently waiting upon the Lord to work, He sent us Alain Moray, a Belgian graduate of the European Bible Institute. Alain had worked with an evangelistic movement for five years in France.

In October 1979, we opened the gospel hall, which we built ourselves in the stable of our old farm house, and Alain was ordained as our pastor. The church now has twenty-five members and a vision to reach the surrounding villages with the gospel.

*****

Maurice Seauve and his wife Nancy had a burden to establish a church in the 17th District of Paris. The following is an account of how the Lord provided their needs.

A church that had dissolved gave their building on a dead end street, in the 17th District of Paris. Starting with an empty building the Lord began to put a congregation together. Maurice and Nancy applied to «FRANCE MISSION.» While waiting for the wheels of the Mission to turn regarding their support, the young couple found an apartment in this section of Paris and moved in. They began to acquaint themselves with this section of Paris, which is largely residential and commercial. It is made up of 200,000 people, including many French aristocrats and many middleclass Parisians, but practically no gospel witness at all.

One cold January day Maurice discovered 400 red velvet seats stacked on the sidewalk outside a theatre. He learned they were to be hauled to the dump and if he wanted some of them, they were his for carrying them away. He chose 75 of the best ones and put them in the empty building.

A few days later as he walked past an office building, he saw gray carpeting and good lumber stacked on the sidewalk. After enquiring about this material, he learned for the second time that the material was his for the carrying away. God's supplying these needs in this unusual way encouraged the Seauves to believe that it was a foretaste of future blessings.

The next step was to invite Christian friends from other churches to a prayer meeting one Sunday afternoon. About eighty people came to pray with them and for them. The following week two couples who had heard about the prayer meeting enquired if a church was going to be organized by the Seauves. They were seeking an evangelical church in the community. They and the Seauves were the first six members of the new church!

Four Bible clubs were organized: one for children,

one for young people, one for ladies and one for senior citizens. Invitations were printed and distributed in the immediate area of the hall. Each month a letter was written, describing special Bible studies. A series of Christian classical concerts were held in the hall. Operation Mobilization sent teams for two consecutive summers, who distributed 60,000 tracts from door to door in the whole area.

Several more individuals joined the three couples and now about forty attend regularly. Maurice has a goal of beginning other Bible cell groups after the church has fifty members enrolled. The Bible groups will be held in the same District and the plan is that once a month they will all join in a monthly rally to keep in touch and to encourage one another.

«And the things thou hast heard among many witnesses, the same commit thou to faithful men, who shall be able to teach others also.»

*****

KJELL JOHANSON   Sweden

For a number of years before the Greater Europe Mission established a Bible Institute in Sweden, a number of Swedish young people came to EBI. Among them was Kjell Johanson, who is presently Assistant Director of the Swedish Bible Institute. Here is Kjell's testimony that he shared with us recently.

I was raised by my grandparents and through my grandmother I came to know the Saviour. One night as a small boy, seven years old, I could not sleep because I felt my need of the Saviour. I got out of bed and kneeled and prayed a simple prayer, «Lord Jesus, please save me.» I then told my family I was saved and went back to bed! It was all very simple and natural, but I was serious and I know the Lord heard my prayer and saved me.

I was baptised at the age of ten and became a member of the church. I loved the Lord, and church attendance became part of my life. However, we had little Bible teaching and I became spiritually discouraged and was tempted to quit the church altogether. Many were talking about the baptism of the Holy Spirit and the fullness of the Holy Spirit, but I saw no results of the Spirit in my own life, and little in the lives of others. It was at this time that I began seriously to study my Bible and I discovered that much of what I had been taught did not seem to have any Biblical basis. I saw that I did not have to work or seek, but to accept the Spirit's fullness, because in Christ God has given me all that I needed, including the fullness of the Holy Spirit. It was mine by faith, and by faith alone.

God brought me into contact with missionaries from the USA. For the first time, I believe, I saw what I considered to be true Christianity demonstrated in their lives. Through personal contact with these missionaries I began to grow in grace and in the knowledge of the Lord Jesus Christ.

In spite of my spiritual struggles I always had the conviction that God wanted me in His service. I realized that I had been resisting God's call and was seeking to run my own life in my own way. Through my missionary friends and the study of God's Word I saw that I belonged to Christ, body, soul and spirit. My friends directed me to the European Bible Institute where I spent three wonderful years. Here are some of the lessons the Lord taught me there:

1) That one can be a Christian without commiting intellectual suicide. For the first time in my life I understood and could believe that the Old Testament

was true, that Moses did write the Pentateuch and why I could believe the Biblical record of the supernatural acts of God in history.

2) I began to see the Bible as an organic whole, that God has a plan for the history of mankind and this plan is revealed in His Word. The Bible courses strengthened my faith in the Bible. I learned I could trust God's Word in a practical way.

3) ESMA was a revelation to me! I had no idea about all the missionary work that was going on in the world. It was as if someone had lifted a window blind and let me look out on the world and see its spiritual needs. The inspiration of the weekly ESMA meetings together with the annual ESMA conference were perhaps the most important things that happened to me during those years of study.

After graduating from EBI I worked for a year in the Swedish Baptist Union's literature department, helping to prepare a weekly magazine. At the end of that year I was invited by the Swedish Bible Institute to join the faculty. My wife Viviann (also an EBI graduate) and I considered this invitation to be an honor and I accepted it.

For several years I taught at SBI while at the same time pastoring a Baptist church. In 1972 we attended Trinity College in Deerfield, Illinois where I received my B.A. and the following year I received my M.A. from Wheaton College. We returned to SBI where I rejoined the faculty.

In the beginning of SBI's history, many in Sweden predicted that the Institute would fail as a non-denominational school. But the Lord has given us the privilege of training many Swedish young people who are serving the Lord all over Sweden and in other countries as well. At this point in time we are praying about and planning a European School of Evangelism, which we hope to open in 1981. It will be a graduate school for Bible School graduates who wish to learn more in the fields of church growth, communications and history of evangelism and revivals. It is the first time to my knowledge that this will be done in Europe and we need much prayer, support, advice and information. The courses will be offered in English and will be open to students from any European country.

I recently attended MISSION 80 before coming over to the USA. During MISSION 80 I often thought of you and how ESMA started under your leadership at EBI. The Lord has certainly honored that humble beginning and I believe this conference was one of the most important ever held in Europe.

To have studied under you at EBI is one of the things that Viviann and I are most thankful to the Lord for. It had a deep impact upon us and changed the course of our lives in a way that makes us stand continually grateful to the Lord. Viviann joins me in sending you and Mrs. Munn our warmest greetings.

Sincerely in Christ,

KJELL

*****

JEAN JACQUES WEILER — France

It has been interesting and exciting to see how God has led in such different ways these young Timothys who came to EBI for training. Their testimonies and the way in which they have assumed leadership within the European Church are indeed accounts of God's power and grace. When one considers how little they knew of the Bible and their limited Christian experience and then to see them become national evangelists, church planters, pastors, and teachers in Bible schools, not to mention a goodly number who went overseas to engage in pioneer missionary work and Bible translation among primitive pagan tribes, one can only give all the glory to Christ and Christ alone. Jean Jacques Weiler is no exception. Here is his story.

Beloved Friends:

What a joy it was to receive your letter and to know you are still active in the Lord's service.

It has been years since our paths have crossed. I believe the Lord used you more than anyone to influence my life. (Please stay humble, dear brother!) I hope our paths may cross. I need a doctrine teacher for our Bible center in Montmeyran. Would you be willing to come and teach from time to time? I hope the following information may be helpful to you.

MY CONVERSION (Not very spectacular)

I was raised in a Christian home and heard the gospel from my early childhood. My father and mother were converted during the war when I was five years old; I still remember the great change that took place in our family. I was converted at the age of ten in a children's Bible camp. At eighteen years I really felt God was calling me into His service, and I wished at that time to enter a Bible School. My father, however, insisted that I do my military service first. The war between France and Algeria was at its height and so I spent thirty-two months of my life in a war situation.

EUROPEAN BIBLE INSTITUTE

During my military service I became more convinced than ever that God wanted me in His service and He would spare me from death. I had heard of EBI's evangelistic and missionary emphasis from Jean Herrgott and also from Ruth Nussbaumer (EBI secretary and my future sister-in-law). I entered the Institute and spent two years of study. How can I enumerate the lessons God taught me? To trust Him for material needs, even a postage stamp, was something I had never done before. The discipline of systematic Bible study was a tremendous blessing to me. I could sum it all up in a single statement. My spiritual life was deepened and my missionary vision enlarged. Also the realization that apart from prayer before, during and after any evangelistic effort was my greatest weakness. I am still faced with this need. Most of all, I got a vision of my own country of France as a mission field.

If I were to share with you all that God has done during these past sixteen years since I engaged in Youth for Christ, I, too, would have to write a book and entitle it «These Sixteen Years!» During these years I have seen God do miracles. Evangelistic teams, high school Bible studies in many schools, annual Bible camps, special teams to evangelize in different regions of France, a Bible training center, which offers young people a concentrated Bible study and practical work, and doors open everywhere for the preaching of the gospel. These are some of the blessings God has bestowed upon us in Youth for Christ, France.

Our budget in 1971 was $2,500. In 1979 it was $270,000, ninety-five per cent of which has come from France. We have been able to contribute 10 % to Youth for Christ International.

We have also been able to purchase an old farm and transform it into a Bible training center. We were obliged to pay $250,000 for this property over a three-year period. At present we only owe $40,000. Praise the Lord! This is the Lord's doings and it is marvellous in our eyes.

We hope to train scores of young people and share our evangelistic vision with them. We have five teams working in Valence, Puy, Avallon, Alsace and Marseilles. Our greatest problem is to find workers who will be willing to pay the price. We have seen many young people come to know Christ and a number of these have already entered Bible schools.

WHAT WE WISH TO SEE ACCOMPLISHED

1) An audio-visual center for all of France.
2) To begin soon our one-year Bible training program: three months of theory and nine months of practical work.
3) To develop Youth for Christ programs in new regions of France.
4) To train French leaders for francophone countries including Canada and Africa.

5) To try to develop strong leadership for the Church of Christ in France.

Finally, we constantly pray that God will keep before us the vision of a lost world, without Christ, for without a vision the people perish.

*****

ERIC GAY   Switzerland

The testimonies of these EBI «Timothys» are not given in their order of importance. The apostle Paul states clearly in Romans 12:5-6, «So we, being many, are one body in Christ and everyone members of one another. Having then gifts differing according to the *grace that is given to us....*» And in I Corinthians 12:11, «But all these (gifts) worketh that one and selfsame Spirit, dividing to every man *severally* as he will.»

Among the gifts of the Spirit is the gift of administration, (ruling, government) Romans 12:8; I Corinthians 12:28 and I Timothy 5:17. The Lord has endowed Eric Gay with unusual ability to organize and administer. When we asked Eric to give us some information concerning his ministry he sent us an hourlong tape. I wish he would write his own testimony as recorded on the tape. It is far too long to include all of it in this chapter. In it he mentioned some of the impossible things that God did through him and his co-workers in organizing two of the largest missionary conferences in the history of Europe. Only eternity will reveal the results of these European Urbana-type conferences, in which thousands of young people made commitments to Jesus Christ. Bible schools registrars enrolled students on the conference site, churches from which the young people came organized missionary prayer meetings for the first time. Missionary information is now going out in eleven different languages, and sent to fifteen thousand people. These are just some of the visible results; only God knows the invisible results of MISSION 76 and MISSION 80.

All this did not happen automatically or without much travail of soul and exercising of faith. In 1974, when Eric booked an office in the Palais de Beaulieu in Lausanne, he had just enough money to pay for one month's rent. He found some pencils and writing paper that had been left over from the Congress on Evangelism that had taken place some months before. In the next several months God would provide several hundred thousand dollars to cover the expenses of MISSION 76.

«But we often had to pray for our daily bread,» Eric wrote me, «and those first EBI graduates who joined me in this venture of faith had to find their support, as well, and this was not easy. But God provided a table in the wilderness and day by day, month by month, God supplied our needs. We learned anew that God's work done in God's way will never lack God's supply. He is faithful and the motto of MISSION 80, HE IS LORD, was demonstrated in the great things God did in the lives of thousands who attended the conference. God gave us new vision, new understanding of his ways, new strengthening of faith, new challenges to commit our lives to Him. How can we enumerate His blessings? They are like the stars of heaven in multitude; they cannot be numbered. We can only say, 'Great is Thy faithfulness.'»

In an official paper sent out after the conference and called MISSION, Eric wrote an

OPEN LETTER TO PARTICIPANTS

Dear Friends:
MISSION 80 opened its doors on December 27, 1979. Within a few hours we saw thousands of people arrive

by coach, car, train and plane. You waited patiently here and there; you calmly complied with all that the administration required of you.

Many of us who have been involved in the organization of the Congress felt very moved. Up until then we had talked of figures, forms, programmes, thousands of beds, and meals to be prepared, but all on paper. Then all of a sudden you arrived - 7,000 of you - an impressive group of young people. We had never seen anything like it. Yet, without even knowing you, we began somehow to see that you were our brothers and sisters in Christ, who had come to MISSION 80 with the desire to really listen to the Lord.

Then we saw you go into the halls, to your accommodation and to the restaurants. We began to get worried when there was a «bottleneck» of 2,000 people for half an hour just when the theatre programme was starting on the morning of the 28th, but this proved to be the only problem of this kind.

We felt very small and very weak when we faced the task before us. We cried out once again to the Lord as we had done many times during the preparation work for MISSION 80. More than at any other time in our lives the words, «Jesus Christ is Lord» were revealed to us. This unshakeable assurance helped us to put our trust completely in the faithfulness of our Master, so that we could say with one voice, «Lord Jesus, MISSION 80 is not our Congress but Your Congress. It is a gathering that you have called together. We ask You to reveal Your glory and Your power to us now.»

Hour by hour, day by day, what had been a theme became for many of us a reality and certainly «Jesus Christ is Lord.» He is the Lord of history; He is the Lord of my life; He holds everything in His hand. God has shown us through His children who gave their testimonies that He is Lord in Europe, in Africa, in Russia, in Cambodia and in America.

It has been estimated that there were 2,500 of you who rose to indicate your decision to commit yourselves to the Lord's service. But the figures are a pale reflection of what happened in the hearts of many. Since Jesus Christ is the Lord of our lives and since He calls His children to His service, we are now praying that MISSION 80 will be the start of a new step forward in prayer and in supporting the missionary work of the Church.

When only six weeks before the Congress we had to make arrangements for 7,000 instead of 3,000 people, we were all convinced that God would have to perform a miracle to make this possible. We can now say, Glory to God for the miracle and also for the 2,000,000 printed pages translated into eleven languages, for the 6,000 beds, for the 35 tons of food distributed without mishap, for the 3,150 group meetings (workshops and seminars) which represented a total of 4,725 hours of group work.

MISSION 80 was such a succession of miracles that it became clear to everyone that the glory and the honor for this victory could be given to God alone. God put us in a position of weakness that we could give all the credit for the success to Him. When we met for a weekend of prayer a few weeks before the Congress, the Lord spoke to us through the account of Gideon's victory over the Midianites (Judges 7). We want each of you to know that we presented ourselves with our pitchers, trumpets and lamps and it was God who did the rest.

Your offerings for the various missionary projects that were presented to you during the Congress amounted to 214,780 Swiss francs (about $120,000).

Your generosity is to the glory of God. We are glad to see how you reacted favorably to the principle of supporting specific missionary projects. On behalf of the committee I thank you.

Eric Gay

How can one ever evaluate the spiritual impact or the subsequent results of a missionary conference like MISSION 80? Only God can.

Thank God He is using young men like Eric Gay and thousands of others who confess that Jesus Christ is Lord of their lives, and who have caught the vision of world evangelization. The Lord is mobilizing His Church, today, in every country for missionary endeavor throughout the world.

Wherefore God also hath highly exalted him, and given him a name which is above every name: That at the name of Jesus every knee should bow, of things in heaven, and things in earth, and things under the earth;

and that every tongue should confess that Jesus Christ is Lord, to the glory of God the Father.

(Philippians 2:9-11)

So what shall we call it? Missionary multiplication? A spiritual chain reaction? A divine principle for world evangelization? Discipling Timothys? I leave the answer to you.

AND THE THINGS THAT THOU HAST HEARD OF ME AMONG MANY WITNESSES THE SAME COMMIT THOU TO FAITHFUL MEN WHO SHALL BE ABLE TO TEACH OTHERS ALSO.

CHAPTER 11

These Forty Years
"And More"

As we have recorded this testimony of God's faithfulness during these forty years, we have been thrilled to see how He has used seemingly inconsequential circumstances to reveal His will and accomplish His purpose in our lives as well as in the lives of others. This was true when God led us to Africa, to the United States, to France, Guatemala, the Republic of Ireland and now to Spain.

Six years ago we had several free months during a furlough and decided to go to San Jose, Costa Rica, to brush up on our Spanish in a language school there. The day before we left Costa Rica at the end of our language course, we were having lunch with a mission leader of the Central American Mission and he casually asked me, «If your mission gave you

237

permission to do it, would you be willing to teach in one of our Bible schools for a year, say in Guatemala?»

His question startled me a little bit. I answered, «Yes, I would be interested but I don't believe the Greater Europe Mission would give me a year's leave of absence to do that.»

The next day we stopped in Guatemala for a four-day visit. Several of the missionaries asked me the same question, could I get permission for a year's leave of absence from GEM to teach in the Guatemala Bible Institute? They were very short staffed and urged us to pray about the possibility. We told them we would be delighted to have such an experience but we were not sure at all that we could get permission from our mission to do it. However, the idea greatly intrigued me, because the Mayan culture found everywhere in Guatemala was so different to anything I had known in Africa or Europe that I found myself wishing I could stay and teach at GBI. So we assured our friends we would pray about it and if it were possible we would return.

The Greater Europe Mission did consent to our going back to Guatemala for a year and we spent a wonderful and blessed year teaching in Chimaltenango at GBI. From there we returned to Europe at the end of 1975 and spent our last year teaching at the Belgian Bible Institute in Heverlee, Belgium, before resigning from GEM. Here again God intervened in our lives in what seemed to be a very insignificant circumstance to lead us to the Republic of Ireland.

Several times we have been asked, «Why did you go to the Republic of Ireland? Did you feel called there?» I have always believed that God calls us to people and not to countries. He sometimes gives certain convictions and engineers circumstances that indicate His leading to certain geographical areas, but

238

Jesus told His disciples to go into ALL THE WORLD and preach the gospel to EVERY CREATURE. Languages, cultures and colors may vary but men's spiritual need of salvation through hearing and accepting Christ's finished work on the cross remains the same everywhere. They must hear in order to believe and receive Christ and be saved but «How can they hear without a preacher and how can they preach except they be sent?» This divine principle has not been changed and the Great Commission given by Christ in Matthew 28:16-20 has never been abrogated. So whether we go across the street or across the seas, we go to proclaim to sinners that «Christ Jesus came into the world to save sinners.» (I Timothy 1:15)

To answer the question, «Why did we go to the Republic of Ireland?» The answer is very simple. A dear friend offered us an apartment rent free for a year! For a number of years I had wanted to complete the series of Bible correspondence courses that I had begun many years before. (See chapter 9, page 189ff) The offer of this apartment for a year, where I could study and complete these courses seemed to be an indication that God was leading us in this direction and so we went to live in Dun Laoghaire (pronounced Dunleary), 10 miles south of Dublin.

When we entered the apartment we almost gasped in surprise. I had been unable to bring my study books from Belgium, and it would be some months, at least, before I could recuperate them. But here in our apartment were about 1400 Bible study books and commentaries, besides several score of Bible studies and messages on cassette tapes. We learned that the owner's husband, who had gone to be with Christ, had been a keen Bible student. He had accumulated this fine library of wonderful, theological books. I said to Betty, «We left one library behind and found another one in Dun Laoghaire.»

We were also informed that our apartment was used three evenings a week to accomodate about thirty Evening Bible School students. The London Bible College held an Extension Bible Study program for the Dublin area and two classes three nights a week were held in the large dining and living rooms of the apartment. We were invited to join the faculty. It was exciting for us to see how wonderfully God led in this decision to go to Ireland and through the simple offer of an apartment opened up a whole new ministry for us.

During the next four years we spent in the Republic of Ireland we were able to write eight new Bible courses to complete the series we had planned on the New Testament. Five of these were printed and are being used throughout Great Britain and English speaking West Africa, especially in Ghana and Nijeria. When we left Ireland in 1979 the Lord laid it upon the heart of a fine missionary couple to continue the ministry of the Personal Bible Studies and God continues to use these studies for His glory. A number of people have professed faith in Christ through the gospel course based on Luke.

When we began to write «These Forty Years» we were not sure what God's will was concerning our immediate future missionary service. We left the Personal Bible Studies in good hands in Ireland. We felt the work we tried to accomplish there was finished. Was it God's will for us once more to return to Europe? Several invitations to work in the USA or in Central America among Spanish speaking people were considered. It was hard to know God's will as we felt ourselves being pulled in various directions.

But again through several seemingly inconsequential circumstances God began to indicate to us that

240

He still has a work for us to do in Europe, where opportunities for witness both in France and Spain are open to us. So we offered our services to the Spanish World Gospel Mission to represent the mission in Spain and to create by God's help a followup program with our Bible correspondence courses for the radio ministry of the Rev. Florent Toirac, Founder and Director of SWGM.

Florent and his wife Dorothy were our missionary colleagues teaching with us at the European Bible Institute, France, in the early fifties. Florent along with his teaching ministry was also responsible for the broadcast in Spanish, called «El Camino de la Vida» - The Way of Life. God so blessed his radio ministry that he felt led of the Lord to launch the Spanish World Gospel Mission, which is presently broadcasting the gospel over 125 radio stations in twenty-six countries throughout the Spanish speaking world. Four years ago we were invited by the SWGM to represent their work in Spain but we had already become involved in missionary work in Ireland and wished to establish the Personal Bible Studies in that land. We knew it would take several years to accomplish this, but we agreed to pray about and consider this proposal sometime in the future. Now the time has come and we look forward in faith to see how God will lead us in this new venture of faith.

As we consider these forty years *and more,* we share the testimony of the hymn-writer when he penned the words:

> How good is the God we adore,
> Our faithful unchangeable friend;
> Whose love is as great as His power
> And knows neither measure nor end.

«For this God is our God for ever and ever; he will be our guide even unto death.» (Psalm 48:14)

HALLELUJAH!